THE
PSYCHOLOGY
OF
PARABLES

DENNIS A. MCINTYRE

FOREWORD

The story of the Prodigal Son, found in the fifteenth chapter of Luke, has been used often in sermons to help people recognize and understand that God is waiting for them with open arms. It tells us that we can make decisions and choose actions that turn us away but that our creator is patiently waiting for us to return. We are told that our choices can lead us to utter despair and when everything we attempt turns to failure, we have a father who welcomes us back with great joy. That joy is so great that our father wants to share it with everyone around.

This parable is a wonderful story of our father's love for his creation, but is that really what it was all about? Jesus came to "seek and save the lost", so it would make sense that this illustration is a form of confirmation. Nevertheless, I believe there is so much more than that. Who was Jesus talking to? Why would he tell that parable to them? What were the conditions that led up to the event? Parables are earthly stories with spiritual significance. Throughout this manuscript answers to these and other questions will be presented for consideration. Perhaps, together we can find some new truths and reasons to celebrate with Jesus.

Jesus used parables as earthly stories with spiritual meanings. This is especially important two thousand years later. Although the stories used common associations of his day, like sheep, lamp oil, or silver coins, we can still apply them to our lives today. In order to fully grasp the eternal implication, however, we need to look at all of the events that led to their sharing. In the process, we may learn a lot about on how to deal with people who have an agenda that is leading them away from eternity with Jesus.

The New International Version (NIV) of the bible is used unless otherwise indicated.

CONTENTS

DENNIS A. MCINTYRE

THE PARABLE OF THE WAYWARD SON

This account has also been referred to as "The Prodigal Son."

Luke 15: 11- 31

11 Jesus continued: "There was a man who had two sons.

12 The younger one said to his father, 'Father, give me my share of the estate.' So he divided his property between them.

13 "Not long after that, the younger son got together all he had, set off for a distant country and there squandered his wealth in wild living.

14 After he had spent everything, there was a severe famine in that whole country, and he began to be in need.

15 So he went and hired himself out to a citizen of that country, who sent him to his fields to feed pigs.

16 He longed to fill his stomach with the pods that the pigs were eating, but no one gave him anything.

17 *"When he came to his senses, he said, 'How many of my father's hired men have food to spare, and here I am starving to death!*

18 I will set out and go back to my father and say to him: Father, I have sinned against heaven and against you.

19 I am no longer worthy to be called your son; make me like one of your hired men.'

20 So he got up and went to his father. "But while he was still a long way off, his father saw him and was filled with compassion for him; he ran to his son, threw his arms around him and kissed him.

21 "The son said to him, 'Father, I have sinned against heaven and against you. I am no longer worthy to be called your son.'

22 "But the father said to his servants, 'Quick! Bring the best robe and put it on him. Put a ring on his finger and sandals on his feet.

23 Bring the fattened calf and kill it. Let's have a feast and celebrate.

24 For this son of mine was dead and is alive again; he was lost and is found.' So they began to celebrate.

25 "Meanwhile, the older son was in the field. When he came near the house, he heard music and dancing.

26 So he called one of the servants and asked him what was going on.

27 'Your brother has come,' he replied, 'and your father has killed the fattened calf because he has him back safe and sound.'

28 "The older brother became angry and refused to go in. So his father went out and pleaded with him.

29 But he answered his father, 'Look! All these years I've been slaving for you and never disobeyed your orders. Yet you never gave me even a young goat so I could celebrate with my friends.

30 But when this son of yours who has squandered your property with prostitutes comes home, you kill the fattened calf for him!'

31 " 'My son,' the father said, 'you are always with me, and everything I have is yours.

32 But we had to celebrate and be glad, because this brother of yours was dead and is alive again; he was lost and is found.' "

"**And Jesus continued**" begins the account. He was talking to a group of people and then shared this parable. If the story was designed to answer a direct question, we could have seen the words, "He answered by telling them this story". If we are to take an honest look at scripture, it is wise to consider the events that led up to it, the participants, the setting, and the culture at the time. We can easily add our own thoughts or applications to scripture to serve our own purposes and at the same time take things way out of context. Therefore, we need to seek answers to some basic questions before coming to any reasonable conclusions. The concept of "seeking" is another of God's rich desires for us to do. So let us seek answers together.

Questions to ponder:

☐ What brought the "Sinners and tax collectors" to hear the words of Jesus?

_____

☐ Who do you think they thought Jesus was?

_____

☐ Read Luke 15: 1 – 3. Is there any indication that the general audience knew why Jesus was sharing parables with them?

_____

☐ Do you think the audience listened to each parable as if it applied directly to them? (Why or why not)

_____

☐ Are there any indications that Jesus planned this encounter?

_____

WHY WAS JESUS SHARING THIS STORY?

If we look back at the beginning of the account, we read these words:

Luke 15: 1 – 3

1 Now the tax collectors and "sinners" were all gathering around to hear him.

2 But the Pharisees and the teachers of the law muttered, "This man welcomes sinners and eats with them."

3 Then Jesus told them this parable: ...

Jesus knew everyone in the audience and every motive in their hearts. He came as God in the flesh. The Jewish religious leaders were muttering (some accounts use the word murmuring) among themselves, regarding the class of people who made up the bulk of Jesus' audience. I can picture these leaders gathering in clusters in the back of the crowd with voices not much higher than a whisper. Jesus had a message for everyone to hear, which focused on the antics and, perhaps, wee voices at the back of the crowd. In one sense, he was performing rumor control. When a rumor gets momentum, it is much harder to stop. In other words, Jesus wanted to address the issue, about why he would speak to an audience of sinners, head on.

Questions to ponder:

☐ How do you think the crowd would have reacted to being referred to as "sinners?"

_____

☐ Do you think the crowd thought of the religious leaders as "righteous" and without sin?

_____

☐ If these leaders came forward and spoke in Jesus place, would they have been given the same reverence?

_____

In addition, Jesus had a short period of time (about three years) to get the message out. His words had eternal significance. Therefore, urgency was necessary, and any defiance needed to be dealt with quickly. We might ask the question, "Why didn't Jesus single out the Jewish leaders and answer their questions directly? This work will take an in depth look at this very question. The more we look into the ministry of Jesus, the more we can learn about how we can deal with others more effectively today. There are times when we need to take a direct stand on an issue. When someone asks about what I believe regarding eternity, I rarely beat around the bush with an answer. I praise God that I live in a country where we have the freedom of expression. Those asking the question do not have to agree, but they will know where I stand. In this account, the muttering came from hearts filled with jealousy and fixed agendas.

A direct answer could be like entering a debate. Jesus could have gathered the leaders aside and held a small meeting, without the rest of the people able to hear what was said, but he chose to address the issue in an indirect way using parables. You will see that Jesus did not tell just one story, but several. The stories involved everyday topics, so those in attendance could relate. With each parable came insights into the very heart of God the Father and Creator. Hearts needed to be prepared to accept each truth. The sequence, which the stories were presented, was significant.

SO WHY USE PARABLES?

Parables were earthly stories with spiritual meanings. Not everyone would understand the meanings. Hearts, which were hardened, could only relate to the tangible account. Hearts that were open to receive the hidden truths, could unlock the secrets with new joy. The audience was filled with hearts that were, at least, willing to receive the message. Many of the religious leaders came with a preconceived purpose to stop Jesus from entering their turf. Their hearts were hard, yet the message was for them as well. They were like a steamroller moving in a path of destruction, which needed to stop, change direction, and clear a new path. If even one heart in this group was open to hear his words, then there would be great joy in heaven. Parables could, therefore, address the issues for everyone, without being outwardly offensive.

Those who heard only the earthly application listened to it as a story. Jesus used several stories in an attempt to lead everyone towards the spiritual truths hidden within. As a technical instructor, I often use multiple examples in order to get the students to understand the materials. One group may grasp the information quickly, while others pick it up later. Some may never get it at all. The use of a series of parables in this account seemed to be aimed directly at the Pharisees and Sadducees, so that they would have a chance to grasp the eternal truth. Jesus loved everyone. These leaders were no different than anyone else, as far as how God valued them.

We will address each parable, along with its significance, throughout this book. Perhaps, in their study we will find new methods in reaching others for the cause of Christ today. We may be seen as the "bull in the china shop" through our aggressive or unrelenting behavior towards others. Often, this approach has only two possible outcomes, and both defeat the purpose. First, we may charge into the wall that separates people from God's truth, in an attempt to knock it down. The wall stays in tact, despite our best effort. In this example we are the ones being hurt, especially in the area of pride. Second, we are able to shatter the wall in one tremendous blow, only to see the people pointing the finger at us for knocking the wall down. In this case, they do not see the truth on the other side. They only focus on rebuilding the wall.

Jesus used parables, much like a chisel. Slowly, he chipped away at the wall until it eventually fell. He was not concerned with how quickly the wall dropped. It was not important that the wall explode like a modern day action movie. The falling of the barrier was necessary to allow the truth on the other side to now be visible. Jesus began to chisel away at the hardened hearts of the Jewish leaders and others. A direct approach would be like:

☐ "You are fools. Don't you get it?"

☐ "What are you murmuring about in the back? If you have something to say, say it to everyone."

These approaches would be like the raging bull with little hope for understanding. The leaders would have put up their horns like most of us, when we are verbally attacked. "Who does he think he's talking to?" may be one response. "We are the authority here. Who does he think he is?" might be another.

Before we begin this study, we may get some initial insight from Jesus, regarding the use of parables.

Consider the "Parable of the Sower" in Matthew.

Matthew 13: 1- 17

1 That same day Jesus went out of the house and sat by the lake.

2 Such large crowds gathered around him that he got into a boat and sat in it, while all the people stood on the shore.

3 Then he told them many things in parables, saying: "A farmer went out to sow his seed.

4 As he was scattering the seed, some fell along the path, and the birds came and ate it up.

5 Some fell on rocky places, where it did not have much soil. It sprang up quickly, because the soil was shallow.

6 But when the sun came up, the plants were scorched, and they withered because they had no root.

7 Other seed fell among thorns, which grew up and choked the plants.

8 Still other seed fell on good soil, where it produced a crop—a hundred, sixty or thirty times what was sown.

9 He who has ears, let him hear."

10 The disciples came to him and asked, "Why do you speak to the people in parables?"

11 He replied, "The knowledge of the secrets of the kingdom of heaven has been given to you, but not to them.

12 Whoever has will be given more, and he will have an abundance. Whoever does not have, even what he has will be taken from him.

13 This is why I speak to them in parables: "Though seeing, they do not see; though hearing, they do not hear or understand.

14 In them is fulfilled the prophecy of Isaiah: " 'You will be ever hearing but never understanding; you will be ever seeing but never perceiving.

15 For this people's heart has become calloused; they hardly hear with their ears, and they have closed their eyes. Otherwise they might see with their eyes, hear with their ears, understand with their hearts and turn, and I would heal them.'

16 But blessed are your eyes because they see, and your ears because they hear.

17 For I tell you the truth, many prophets and righteous men longed to see what you see but did not see it, and to hear what you hear but did not hear it.

The disciples asked Jesus a direct question in verse ten; "Why do you speak to the people in parables? Jesus may have spoke to them in a more direct manner, so this new approach may have seemed odd. Nevertheless, Jesus answered their question directly. He told the disciples that they had the knowledge of the secrets of the kingdom of heaven, but this knowledge was not to those with calloused hearts. The parable of the sower was for the disciples to understand, but a mystery to the audience without a change of heart. Jesus then unlocked the mystery for all to hear.

Matthew 13: 18 –22

18 "Listen then to what the parable of the sower means:

19 When anyone hears the message about the kingdom and does not understand it, the evil one comes and snatches away what was sown in his heart. This is the seed sown along the path.

20 The one who received the seed that fell on rocky places is the man who hears the word and at once receives it with joy.

21 But since he has no root, he lasts only a short time. When trouble or persecution comes because of the word, he quickly falls away.

22 The one who received the seed that fell among the thorns is the man who hears the word, but the worries of this life and the deceitfulness of wealth choke it, making it unfruitful.

23 But the one who received the seed that fell on good soil is the man who hears the word and understands it. He produces a crop, yielding a hundred, sixty or thirty times what was sown."

Each member of the audience heard the meaning of the parable, and would have to examine their heart. If they truly understood, then the words of Jesus took root and flourished. They could hear his words, but later choke them out with worry or greed. Jesus warns that persecution will come, because of Jesus. In order for the word to prosper, persecution would have to be endured. This truth is still true today. The disciples became sowers.

There is another point to consider for this parable. The farmer scattered the seed across all types of soil. He did not examine the soil first to limit where the seeds would fall. He did not throw the seed sparingly. Jesus carried out this principle as he spoke to all people. He used parables so that each listener could not unlock the hidden meanings without discernment. The words of Jesus were planted with the hope that all would grow. Jesus knew that fertile soil was not plentiful, but his word must be spread, regardless. Sowing is the responsibility of all believers. It is not limited to the pulpit on Sundays. Seeds of hope need to be planted daily in the lives of everyday people with everyday burdens and concerns. Jesus taught his disciples this principle then and it still holds true today.

My first published book, called "Legacy of Love," was originally meant for my family. It told the story of my father who suffered great loss, blamed

God, and reconciled with Jesus at the age of eighty-nine. Along with capturing dad's legacy, I shared what it was like growing up without a mother from an emotional point of view. During my wife's battle with cancer seven years later, God convinced me that the book was to be distributed to the world. Many people who read it had told me that I should publish, but I brushed the thought aside. After my wife passed away, I knew that I had to seek publication. When I received my first copies, I gave a few to friends. I did not realize that hidden within the words were my childhood feelings, which touched the hearts of my new readers. I received word from one family who reunited after years of emotional separation. Another divorcee read it and passed her copy on to her ex-husband. After more than eight years, which is as long as I knew the lady, they remarried. God was doing amazing things with a story meant for my family.

Since publication, I began to capture everyday accounts of people that I met in coffee houses. I titled the work, "Coffee Shop Ministries." The stories were placed on a friend's website, one per month. The site owner started receiving an unusually high number of hits and email asking for more stories. Somehow, the stories seemed to have a heartbeat. Readers were being uplifted. I pondered the question, "Why were my stories touching hearts. They were about everyday people sharing a cup of coffee." Then it hit me. People are going through many setbacks in life. They often feel alone and helpless. They could relate to the characters in my stories. Although some may be in despair, it was my hope that they left in a better frame of mind. Readers felt relief from their struggles while they read. The fact that many readers took the time to email back to the website's manager is a testimony to the impact the stories had upon them.

Golfers tend to perk their ears up, when golf stories are shared nearby. Moms may react in a similar manner, when childhood antics are the subject. One of the key methods of helping people suffering from some form of addiction involves group therapy, where they can relate to others going through the same things. The human race has a spiritual and emotional side, different from other life forms. Animals may have more acute sensing in the areas of smell, hearing, or sight. However, they are less sensitive to feelings of the heart. They are not found studying the solar system to find where they came from. A pet may sense sadness with an owner and come to them, but it cannot relate to the cause.

Jesus addresses the issues of the heart in his parables. He loves all of us without exception, and his love is not measured on a scale of one to ten. We are all tens. We need to make Jesus a ten as well. Marriages, based on a fifty-fifty relationship are headed for disaster. Yet, this concept is close to the norm. Jesus did not come to give his life for us If we did something in return. He gave it because he loves us unconditionally. He gave one hundred percent. He held back nothing. His message to the disciples was to sow seeds of truth and hope everywhere. Do not hold back. Do not reserve his words for a close circle of friends or family members alone. The world consists of every type of heart (soil) that needs to hear about love, joy, and peace. Every heart has a longing to receive that message, unless it has shut (hardened) its doors.

So how does this relate to the parables of Jesus? People long to hear good news. The news media tends to focus on just the opposite. Jesus spoke about the greatest good news that the world would ever hear, namely, a relationship with him in the kingdom of heaven for all eternity. It was hard enough for the world to understand things it could see, but the unseen was like a mystery. People yearn for relief from pain, sickness, sorrow or grief. Drugs, alcohol, or pleasure tend to treat the symptoms, but the feelings return. Reading everyday accounts of people facing similar obstacles, but with fruits of joy or peace, offers a more lasting relief. The seeds we can plant come from the fruit we are producing. The stories we can share are our testimonies. We may not have spiritual truths hidden behind our words, but we have the love of Christ. Miracles are happening daily. God is alive and well. He is working in the lives and hearts of everyday people.

Try visiting a coffee shop or fast food location on any given morning. It has been my experience that people gather on a regular basis to share with one another. It can be amazing to watch. You may see a change in behavior. Smiles and laughter may suddenly erupt without warning. Be prepared as it can be contagious. Everyday events need to be shared. Jesus does not want us to hide in our homes. He desires for us to go to the uttermost parts of the earth and spread the good news. We don't need to be ordained. Our joy in knowing Jesus should be expressed on our faces. We don't need a specific agenda. The Holy Spirit can handle that quite well. The adage, "One man's junk is another man's treasure" may also apply to those everyday events in our lives that brought momentary joy, and have since passed. Sharing those accounts with others keeps them current in our minds and hearts, while becoming a new source of joy for a stranger.

Jesus faced a group of inquisitive people near the Sea of Galilee. The crowd was so large that he had to enter a boat and row away from the shore to address them. Many were there out of curiosity, based on stories or rumors passed down about the man called Jesus. Others were there, because the accounts threatened their livelihood. These people came with more critical attitudes. Let's look at the way Jesus handled his critics, and observe how the chisel began to shape the lives of all the hearts in attendance. Perhaps, we may find the hidden truths that we need today.

Questions to ponder?

☐ What memories do you have that bring a smile each time you remember them?

_____

☐ Who else has heard?

_____

☐ Why does Jesus refer to the heart as "calloused?"

_____

WHO WERE IN THE AUDIENCE?

Tax Collectors and Sinners

Tax collectors and sinners were gathered to hear Jesus. It is interesting that these groups are mentioned separately. Romans 3:23 tells us "**All have sinned and fall short of the glory of God**". Tax collectors were just as human as everyone else there. On the surface the separation between sinners and tax collectors may seem strange. We are introduced to two other groups that help to put the pieces together, namely the Pharisees and teachers of the law. Were these groups separate as well? To fully understand the events, we need to understand all of the participants, the culture, and the underlying hierarchy of that day.

Zacchaeus the Tax Collector

Luke 19:1-10

1 Jesus entered Jericho and was passing through.

2 A man was there by the name of Zacchaeus; he was a chief tax collector and was wealthy.

3 He wanted to see who Jesus was, but being a short man he could not, because of the crowd.

4 So he ran ahead and climbed a sycamore-fig tree to see him, since Jesus was coming that way.

5 When Jesus reached the spot, he looked up and said to him, "Zacchaeus, come down immediately. I must stay at your house today."

6 So he came down at once and welcomed him gladly.

7 All the people saw this and began to mutter, "He has gone to be the guest of a 'sinner.' "

8 But Zacchaeus stood up and said to the Lord, "Look, Lord! Here and now I give half of my possessions to the poor, and if I have cheated anybody out of anything, I will pay back four times the amount."

9 Jesus said to him, "Today salvation has come to this house, because this man, too, is a son of Abraham.

10 For the Son of Man came to seek and to save what was lost."

Luke talks about another encounter with a tax collector in chapter nineteen. His name was Zacchaeus. Verse two says that he was "a chief tax collector and he was wealthy." He was a very short man who wanted to see Jesus so bad that he ran ahead and climbed a sycamore fig tree. Jesus saw him, told him to come down **immediately** from the tree, and went to his house to eat with him. Verse six says, "So he came down **at once** and welcomed him **gladly**."

Not all of the tax collectors of that day were wealthy, but they were regarded by the religious leaders as outcasts of society and not to be associated with. I have always wondered, whether tax collectors frequented the church. Were they outcasts, because they handled money with an element of greed? Apparently, they were lower than the classification called "sinners." Suppose, tax collectors gave regular tithes to the church. Would they still be held at the bottom of the totem pole in stature? Whatever the reason, tax collectors were not well liked by the religious leaders of that day. However, the crowd of people did not seem to have the same lack of respect. Tax collectors were mixed with everyone else. The account does not depict a riotous mob trying to remove Zacchaeus from the tree as he climbed to get above them to see Jesus. When Jesus acknowledged Zacchaeus, the crowd was more interested in what Jesus had to say, then who Zacchaeus was. That, certainly, was not the agenda for the religious leaders.

In this account we see an attitude of excitement or joy, with respect to being in an audience in front of Jesus. Jesus added an emphasis that can easily be overlooked when he said to Zacchaeus' **"I must stay at your house today"**. The religious leaders would, certainly have taken note of these words. Not only is Jesus staying with lowly tax collectors, but insists on it. Zacchaeus, however, may have rejoiced in his heart with the same words. I question, whether Jesus would have received a warm welcome to stay at one of the religious leader's home?

Zacchaeus responded without hesitation and welcomed Jesus with sincere joy. Zacchaeus so eagerly sought to get a glimpse of the one who brought a new message of hope, that he climbed a tree. He was too short to see over the taller crowd, so he took action. Perhaps, He stood out to Jesus, because he elevated himself above the crowd. Nevertheless, Jesus spotted Him. Then, Jesus spoke directly to Zacchaeus, despite the throngs of people all around. His words were heard by many in attendance, but pierced one man's heart who eagerly sought Jesus. Jesus knew the heart of the man climbing the tree. It was a heart filled with expectation. The one coming had a message meant for him. Somehow, Zacchaeus had heard about Jesus, and with great excitement he ran to see him. His stature in the community or physical height did not keep him from the goal of seeing Jesus with his own eyes. He was like a needle in a haystack, yet, Jesus singled Zacchaeus out when he reached the tree. Zacchaeus was no longer the small fish in the big pond. He received a personal invitation from the Savior of the whole world.

What a picture! Zacchaeus must have heard about the works and messages preceding Jesus' entry into His town. The life Zacchaeus had as a tax collector may have brought him financial rewards, but there was something about the news of Jesus that seemed to excite him more than money. He ran to the place where Jesus would pass to get a firsthand account of what the hoopla was all about. His curiosity quickly turned to elation, as he received the personal invitation to have Jesus as a guest in his home.

Today, Jesus stands at the door of our hearts knocking, but will we let him in? His invitation has been extended to you and me. Zacchaeus seemed to have His arms open wide to receive Jesus. This picture should be etched in our minds today. Each of us needs to have the same sense of urgency as Zacchaeus, as no one knows what tomorrow brings. When we leave this earth, the door to our eternal home with Jesus is either open or closed, based on our choice. If we invite Jesus into our hearts, then His arms will be open wide to receive us for all eternity.

Rev. 3:20

Here I am! I stand at the door and knock. If anyone hears my voice and opens the door, I will come in and eat with him, and he with me.

Jesus went to anyone who would listen. He not only cared about everyone, but he loved each of them more than life itself. Jesus spoke to the crowds with a message of joy and new hope. His earthly ministry was meant to provide instruction about an eternity with him, which goes well beyond anything they could have imagined. From the beginning of Creation, Jesus knew what his mission would be, and now he is fulfilling it. Man was created in the "image of God" to worship the Creator. This required that man had the ability to make decisions. It also meant that man would choose wrong paths, which needed to be corrected. The crowds followed Jesus, partially because of the miracles they had witnessed, but also because they had a yearning in their hearts to follow on the right path.

Jesus was about to turn the world upside down. The last shall be first, and the first shall be last. The pecking order of status, as viewed from the religious leaders will be reversed. Those, deemed to be on the bottom, will be brought to the head of the class. A servant's heart is seen above a master. The more you have, the more that will be taken away. Sinners and tax collectors can now have a high place of honor in the kingdom of heaven, if they repent and follow Jesus. Jealousy, greed, or haughtiness becomes stumbling blocks to the new order. A part of the mystery of this new kingdom is being revealed to those in his audience, but not all would filly understand. In fact, the secrets would only be unlocked by a select few.

Jesus shared with them as if they were members of his earthly family. There were no amplifiers or elaborate speaker systems. His words would reach each heart, despite the large crowds. I can picture the audience hanging on every word. The dropping of a pin may have sounded like a loud clang. The words, Jesus would share with them, were meant to let them know how much they were loved. Many people may have questioned, "Is this the promised Messiah?" They may have listened with such intent, that their earthly woes might be replaced with a brighter future. Hearts, which come to him full of expectation and excitement, will leave even more joyous. Yet, the concept of eternity and heaven were, probably, remote from their thoughts. The religious leaders did not look upon Jesus as the promised one, but rather as someone who would challenge their own authority.

Questions to ponder:

☐ Jesus was not dressed any differently than those who gathered to hear him speak. Does the clothes a man wears offer any attraction today?

☐ Firsthand accounts of Jesus' miracles may have been spread throughout that land prior to his coming. Are we so eager to seek miracle workers today?

☐ The Jewish leaders were there to protect their agendas, while lesser classes seemed to desire good news that would improve their life. What message was Jesus sending when he called out a tax collector by name and invited himself into their house in a sense of urgency (must)?

It is relatively easy to talk about something we can see with our eyes or touch with our hands. Jesus would use everyday things to describe areas of eternal significance. The teachers of the Law were about to question Jesus as to why he chose to eat with those low on the economic totem pole, rather than eat with the established leadership. If Jesus would talk about spiritual areas, then it would make sense that he talk to those in charge. I can only imagine, the throng of people following a carpenter's son for words of comfort and wisdom must have enraged the spiritual leaders. Their robes were colorful and easily recognizable. Yet, the people followed someone who looked like another one of them. The leaders had achieved a measure of respect, and their status was about to be shattered. To refer to these followers as "sinners and tax collectors," certainly implied that they were part of the bottom echelon of society. Jesus measured mankind with a far different stick. Humility was a virtue. The Pharisees needed to understand something about humility.

In Luke 5:30 Jesus was asked the same question of the Pharisees namely, "Why do you eat with tax collectors and sinners?"

Luke 5:31

Jesus answered them, "It is not the healthy who need a doctor, but the sick. I have not come to call the righteous, but the sinners to repentance."

We don't know, whether any of the same Pharisees who questioned him in this account were there on this day, but we do know that the question was still on their minds. Perhaps, they heard the words spoken by Jesus, but were confused, as the answer did not fit their mold. To them the people who gathered were the ones who were sick. Of course they were the "righteous." Sinners needed to change their ways and repent. Certainly, Jesus was not referring to those defending the law.

The idea of challenging authority is not new. History is full of such events. The United States of America began as a colonial outreach from across the ocean. It meant that people would leave their homes in England for a new start. Religious persecution caused many to jump at the opportunity to find relief. The Declaration of Independence and Bill of Rights established a government "for the people and by the people," which has provided the relief. The founders of America gave everything for the cause of freedom from the tyranny of authority. This writer believes, that this country has been blessed beyond earthly measure as a result. Although Christianity was the predominant faith of the founders, the Constitution provided for every individual to make a personal choice without discrimination.

It seems as though the twenty-first century America is challenging the establish authority, and Christianity is the target audience. The Ten Commandments are being removed from public places. The use of the words "under God" in the country's Pledge of Allegiance offends non-believers. Atheists have been successful in having words removed or changed that imply the existence of God; as such words restrict their freedom to believe that God does not exist.

Personally, I find it rather strange, that atheists are using so much energy to enhance their cause. First, if God does not exist, then what difference does it make if the name is used? Removing the name only removes the hope for those who do believe. For unbelievers, there is no hope or eternity. To focus on seeing the name of God removed from authoritative documents, not only offends the intentions of those who gave their lives to establish this great country, but also seems to have no positive gain. It would be more productive to use the energy promoting such literary deletion to better use, like finding a cure for cancer.

Second, it takes a much higher amount of faith to believe that God does not exist. Even Charles Darwin could not explain how the human eye could reproduce itself, along with other examples in nature. Although, Darwin tried to link everything in human existence to evolution, he still could not explain many things outside of a creator. To believe that everything in life is a result of pure chance, takes great faith indeed.

Third, history has demonstrated that great nations rise from a strong resolve or purpose. America is one example. History also shows that strength comes from within, and countries fall, quickly, from internal decay. The United States of America drew upon the wisdom of its founders to develop the Constitution, which has served the country well for over two centuries. To believe that God does not exist is a right that is defended. If God does exist, then the establishment of a nation based on the words "under God" almost certainly warrants an additional amount of blessing from the Creator. If God does not exist, then removing the words is a mute point. Therefore, it may be better to let a "sleeping dog lie" than disturb it. If God exists, then removing these words may start an avalanche of woes by the removing of the added blessings bestowed.

Jesus stirred the political events of his day. Those who studied the Law knew of a promised Messiah from the writings. Prophets foretold of his coming and yet the religious leaders had blinders on. They were more concerned about their stature than the Law's content. Today, we have the Bible, declared as God's Word. The Old Testament is filled with rituals, instructions, guidelines, and prophecies that the religious leaders in Jesus' day so adamantly protected. Yet, Jesus lets us know that he came, not to condemn the Law, but to fulfill it.

Matthew 5: 17
"Do not think that I have come to abolish the Law or the Prophets; I have not come to abolish them but to fulfill them.

Jesus did not attempt to do away with the Law, but rather to change the way it would be enforced. The religious leaders needed to recognize new responsibilities. They no longer needed to be interpreters. Jesus fulfilled that role as a living Savior. He became the atonement for sin once and for all. It would be hard to fault the leaders, whose jobs were suddenly turned upside down. The career path, they chose to defend the laws of God, now required a new direction. Everything they had worked for reached an unveiling. Instead of seeing a book of how-to instructions, they were now seeing the final work in Jesus. The people could touch, feel, see, and hear their Messiah.

Romans 8: 1-4

1 Therefore, there is now no condemnation for those who are in Christ Jesus,

2 because through Christ Jesus the law of the Spirit who gives life has set you free from the law of sin and death.

3 For what the law was powerless to do because it was weakened by the sinful nature, God did by sending his own Son in the likeness of sinful humanity to be a sin offering. And so he condemned sin in human flesh,

4 in order that the righteous requirement of the law might be fully met in us, who do not live according to the sinful nature but according to the Spirit.

The Law dealt with the problem of sin. Jesus would face the cross to deal with the problem head on. The responsibilities of the ordained leaders, to represent the people and provide sacrifices on their behalf, would soon be done away with. Instruction would soon come from the Spirit of God that dwells in all who believe and receive. The job description of the Jewish leaders was about to be eliminated. They could either look for a new line of work or rebel.

Perhaps, we might have made similar choices in their shoes. The twenty-first century has continually made changes in the workplace. Businesses, which have been around for decades, are being forced to make broad changes to remain economically stable. Old jobs are being eliminated. New skills for the future are sought. Changing jobs multiple times in a career is the norm. The human tendency is to fight the change and cling to the life we know. That is what the Pharisees and Sadducees were doing. Jesus appeared to be leading their followers away. If left unchecked, they would be out of work.

I find it interesting that tax collectors and sinners were the key descriptors for those following Jesus. Rebellion from God is what makes us "sinners." The failure to accept that Jesus was the promised Messiah is a form of rebellion by the religious leaders. Although, all of us are sinners, tax collectors unknowingly categorized themselves with the same label as Jesus' followers. The roll of tax collectors would not be eliminated, but rather improved. These people were regarded as society's bottom feeders, due to dishonest practices. The work of collecting taxes would continue in the earthly kingdom. Jesus was looking for "soul collectors" for a new kingdom, not of this world.

Questions to ponder:

☐ Are there any areas of rebellion from God in your heart?

_____

☐ Are there any areas in your life where you feel God's pull in a new direction?

_____

☐ Do you believe that your country is headed closer or further away from God in the direction it has taken?

_____

PHARISEES

Pharisees were considered the protectors of the law. While under the domination of the Greeks in the third century BC, many Jews were being influenced to accept the pagan religious customs of their captors. A group of Jewish men felt convicted to preserve their heritage and protect the laws handed down from the days of Moses. Their rise to upper status, as religious leaders in Israel, convinced many countrymen to protect their national integrity with a strict adherence to the Mosaic law. Although their intentions were honorable, each successive generation of Pharisees used their influence to make deviations to the law. Greed, self-righteousness, and hypocrisy were their trademarks by the time Jesus came on the scene.

The two centuries of preservation by the Scribes and Pharisees led to many changes and interpretations to the law as it was handed down. America has seen over two hundred years of change. What started out as the preservation of God's values, has become a serious problem from God's perspective. Change, in itself, is not a bad thing. CDs of the twenty-first century are a vast improvement over the eight-track-tapes of the twentieth. The same might be said about automobiles or appliances. Scripture tells us, however, that God is unchanging.

Hebrews 13:8

Jesus Christ is the same yesterday and today and forever.

If God's laws are good, then changing them seems to be a step in the wrong direction. If God wanted his guidelines for all creation to only be relevant for a period in time, then he might send a new set of rules or take judgment on those who broke them. The concept of sending new rules limits the omnipotence of the creator. The test of time is the best measure of anything that hast lasting or eternal value. The original laws from God are as relevant today as they were then. Can we say the same about man's laws today? Is God judging our country based on our obedience to his laws?

Let's take a look at the world we are in. "Thou shall not kill" has been modified to allow women to have the right to kill their unborn child. God's law was pretty simple and direct. Man's law is far more complicated. The issue of when life begins and when a fetus is to be considered as human is a big part of the debate. God says that he knew us before we were born, indicating that our life did not begin when we exited the womb, but while we were still in it. This issue has divided America in about the same amount of time as the good intentions of the Pharisees led to Christ's return (200 years). Christ came to fulfill the original law and end the ritualistic requirements that were handed down. One might wonder what another two hundred years would bring.

The religious leadership to date had added hundreds of modifications. We can surmise that the next two hundred years would raise the ritualistic requirements to thousands of amendments and addendums. I remember playing a game, where someone would whisper something into the person's ear beside him or her, and then tell that person to pass it on. It would not take many people in a line to totally change the message. As an engineer, I would design manufacturing equipment, which would be implemented to produce consumer products. Over time, small modifications needed to be made to improve quality or production rates. It was not unusual to visit the site, where the equipment was being used, and hardly recognize the original designed software program. The changes may have been necessary, since I am only human. I could not anticipate every future scenario. That is not true for an omnipotent, unchanging, and omnipresent God. He is the "Alpha" and the "Omega," the beginning and the end. Changes from his Creation could only be detrimental. His plan foresaw the future, unlike anything I could create. Death came into the world, only after man tried to change the script. The "righteous" of that day, not only changed the law, but closed their hearts and minds to the one who came to fulfill it.

God's prophet, Jeremiah, records the following verse, identifying that it was the "Word of the Lord:"

Jer. 1:5

"Before I formed you in the womb, I knew (or chose) you, before your were born I set you apart"

God let Jeremiah know that he was set apart for a purpose, before he breathed his first breathe of air. He also lets us know that we are no accident. Our earthly lives prepare us for an eternity, based on the choices we make. Ultimately, we either build an intimate relationship with our creator or we reject him. Either way we are the ones responsible for the choices made. Jeremiah lets us know that since we are known by God before we are born, then we can be set apart to be used by God.

Ephesians 2:10

For we are God's workmanship, created in Christ Jesus to do good works, which God prepared in advance for us to do.

Offshoots of the issue of abortion are even more alarming, from God's perspective. Killing a fetus and then taking the body to a lab for embryo research must cause the creator enormous pain. Where is man headed?

☐ Man seems to look for ways to live forever. God has been crying out for man to live forever with him in eternity.

☐ Man says they should have choices like the right to abort. God says that man has choices and hopes that he makes the right ones.

- ☐ Man says marriage is not a lifelong commitment. God says that he will return to take his bride to be with him forever (Rev.21).

- ☐ Man desires to be served. God desires that man serve.

- ☐ Man desires abundance. God says those, "Whose life consists in the abundance of his possessions, is a fool." (Luke 12:14)

"Thou shall not commit adultery" or "Covet your neighbor" are commandments that have new meaning today in society. Generations of single parent households seem to be increasing with over fifty-percent divorce rates in America.

In business we can see similar trends. How a worker looks at another can be taken as an unlawful act. Unions were created to protect workers and now companies are folding their doors because of their demands. It seems as though that, which was created as something good throughout society has degraded to something far less desirable. People are far more ready to condemn than to offer solutions to problems. Values are compromised in lieu of status quo.

Then we can look at education and see the same patterns. The right for everyone to pray is seen as an infringement on the rights of those who don't believe in prayer. Our forefathers placed the "Ten Commandments" in public institutions as a reminder to all on the rules of conduct the country was founded. Now they are being removed by a society who ignores those rules. Evolution has been taught as a science rather than a theory, yet alternative theories are not considered that have evidence to support them. Personally, the engineer in me takes exception to this. We have about 6000 years of evidence and somehow come up with the "theory" that we evolved from apes over billions of years of life. That's like reading the first word in "War and Peace" and accurately predicting every detail and outcome within it. How absurd can we be?

The process of making changes to the Jewish law, set the stage for Jesus to come to earth. We no longer need a priest to go before God and shed blood (sacrifices) on our behalf. The blood of Jesus paid that price once and forever.

Jesus was about to become the High Priest for everyone through the innocent sacrifice of his own life. The curtain that allowed only priests to enter into the "Holy of Holies" was rent. All the promises in the law were fulfilled in that act. Not only that, but his coming was foretold in the very scriptures that the Pharisees were protecting, changing, and enforcing. Perhaps, things might have been different if those charged with copying text had the gift of discernment, and also understood what they were copying. The more times documents are passed, the less the original intent is captured. A business run by e-mail rarely gets anything done, yet those who send the messages often feel they are in control as managers.

The Pharisees had an agenda to defend their position in society at all costs. Jesus came as a threat to their very existence. Up to now, they dictated who, what, when, where, and how eternal things would be handled. In one brief time on earth, Jesus put these things into human form. Those who came to hear him with open hearts, left with new hope. I can picture them running to tell anyone who would listen. They may not have understood beyond the earthly application of Jesus message, but Jesus made an impact, nonetheless. The Pharisees were like rocky soil. Perhaps, there were some who heard Jesus' message and found the same joy as many of the "sinners." Jesus certainly welcomed them.

Questions to ponder:

☐ Have the laws in our country been improved or do they contradict the intentions of our founders?

_____

☐ What roles do lawyers have in our society today? _

_____

☐ When choices do we have when a legal precedence contradicts God's moral standards?

_____

SADDUCEES

Sadducees were a small but powerful group of religious leaders at the time of Jesus. They followed only the Old Testament law. They did not obey the rules added by the Pharisees. The Sadducees did not believe in any life after death. Like the Pharisees, they were often in conflict with Jesus. Even during Jesus' day, there were two opposing groups in the leadership of the church. It was a form of democracy, where checks and balances would keep any one group from taking over like an anarchy.

They were considered priests and, like the Pharisees, had elevated stature in the community. They seemed to have equal standing with the Pharisees, but both groups were in conflict with the authority of Jesus. One difference between the two groups was how they looked at life after death. The Sadducees did not believe in heaven as a place for eternal residence after death. They believed that the soul perished with the body. The Pharisees believed that the soul was eternal. Paul addresses this in one account in the book of Acts.

Acts 23: 1-8

1 Paul looked straight at the Sanhedrin and said, "My brothers, I have fulfilled my duty to God in all good conscience to this day."

2 At this the high priest Ananias ordered those standing near Paul to strike him on the mouth.

3 Then Paul said to him, "God will strike you, you whitewashed wall! You sit there to judge me according to the law, yet you yourself violate the law by commanding that I be struck!"

4 Those who were standing near Paul said, "You dare to insult God's high priest?"

5 Paul replied, "Brothers, I did not realize that he was the high priest; for it is written: 'Do not speak evil about the ruler of your people.'"

6 Then Paul, knowing that some of them were Sadducees and the others Pharisees, called out in the Sanhedrin, "My brothers, I am a Pharisee, the son of a Pharisee. I stand on trial because of my hope in the resurrection of the dead."

7 When he said this, a dispute broke out between the Pharisees and the Sadducees, and the assembly was divided.

8 (The Sadducees say that there is no resurrection, and that there are neither angels nor spirits, but the Pharisees acknowledge them all.)

The Sadducees also did not bow down to the whims of the Pharisees. They did not obey the add-on rules to the law, which the Pharisees instituted. They represented the elite group of people who could enter the "Holy of Holies" inside the temple. They performed the ritualistic services pertaining to sacrifice for the sins of the people. Sadducees were considered God's priests. Even those standing nearby acknowledged that Paul was insulting "God's high priest."

Paul's account also addresses another difference between Sadducees and Pharisees regarding spiritual beings. Sadducees believed that they did not exist. They placed their focus on the first five books of the Bible as the law of Moses.

In contrast, the Pharisees believed acknowledged the presence of angels. They often personified them with wings and the ability to appear at any time and any place. Both groups held firm to their interpretations and were often locked in dispute.

One thing both groups had in common was their ego. They were zealous in their role as caretakers and defenders of the law. Though they disagreed with each other on interpretation, they stood side by side in defending their authority on God's Word. Jesus came along and the initial curiosity turned into rage against Him. Their status as religious leaders was being challenged. I picture a cat with all of its hairs straight and ready to pounce. To them, Jesus was speaking blasphemy and it raised their dander.

Pharisees and Sadducees had their differences to be sure. They were zealous in defending their beliefs, but when Jesus entered the scene, these two groups united with a common cause, namely, to put an end to the blasphemy. They considered themselves to be the righteous spiritual leaders. Now they were seeing flocks of followers seeking the council of Jesus. They were enraged. Whatever differences they had over theology, were now secondary issues. Jesus was a threat and needed to be silenced.

Questions to ponder:

☐ What are the roles of priests today? (Note: priests can be any member of a clergy)

_____

☐ Do we need outward acts of sacrifice to receive forgiveness from God for our sins today?

_____

☐ How should we look at the first five books of the Bible today?

_____

SCRIBES

Another group in the inner circle of spiritual matters were the Scribes. They studied, interpreted, and copied the scriptures. They could have been the "Teachers of the law" described in this account in Luke. Scribes were chosen at the beginning of the Jewish nation to protect and pass on the spiritual inheritance. Again this was a noble profession that became prideful, self-centered, and very influential. Their agenda may have seemed quite different to the people than that of the Sadducees and Pharisees. That sounds like the political arena today. We might consider the Supreme Court doing the work of modern day scribes.

When America was founded, farmers from each state donated a year of their time to represent their state in Washington D.C. It was considered an honor and a privilege. At the same time it was often a hardship, as the family's crops still required harvesting, and the cows needed milking with dad away. These representatives did not have a self-centered agenda but fervently desired to listen to the others and make changes that were for the good of all. They represented their individual state's needs, yet proudly considered themselves Americans first. They brought ideas, placed them on the congressional table, and then synergized with the group to come up with solutions far better than their own, most of the time. What started out as "...of the people, by the people, and for the people" may be quoted today as "...of the influential, by the arrogant, and for the special interest groups." Don't get me wrong here. We have many dedicated and honest representatives in government positions. Yet, it seems as though the ones we hear about in the media are the ones making the loudest noise against the current administration, without anything concrete to offer in the form of a solution. The adage: "If you're not part of the solution, you're part of the problem," holds true. Our forefathers recognized, that in order to move forward, people needed to work collectively together.

God must be looking down on this country's political nightmare today and ready to scream, "Get back to the basics people." Two parties are so diametrically opposed that synergy is nearly impossible. Pointing fingers with malicious intent, while not offering any concrete ways to make improvements are the characteristic of one side. Meeting in the middle on issues would be a welcome relief for the other side. The old idea that when we point a finger at someone, we have three others pointing at us comes to mind here. The murmuring among the religious leaders and teachers of the law may well be compared to politicians today, who seek out those who agree with their points of view in order to get support. One thing was consistent between the Scribes, Sadducees, and Pharisees back then. They could not stand anyone who opposed their work, their teachings, and the law.

We could look at these verses from the perspective of the Pharisees instead of God's perspective. Often emphasis on a subject involves repetition. The same could be said for people. We could also conclude that there were differences between the Pharisees and teachers. From their view, there was a separation between sinners and tax collectors. Nevertheless, they are part of an interesting audience, ranging from the lowest to the highest in the economic order of that day.

Questions to ponder:

☐ The Supreme Court has a charge to defend our constitution. Do you believe that is still true based on their actions?

_____

☐ Can you cite any Supreme Court decisions that have changed the intent of the Constitution and founders of this country?

_____

☐ Can you cite any decisions that our founders would have approved?

_____

☐ Do you think that some added statutes have outlived the purpose originally intended?

_____

☐ Do you feel that the documents established by our founders reflected an honest, unified, and sincere set of fundamentals that were pleasing to God?

_____

☐ Do you think God is pleased with the laws of this land today?

_____

DENNIS A. MCINTYRE

THE INSIGHTS OF JESUS

Now that we know something about his listeners, we also have insights in Jesus' motives. The Pharisees and the teachers of the law "muttered." Remember those school days when classes were disrupted by those conversations in the back of the room. The presentation of the instructor took a back seat to the murmuring and most likely fell on deaf ears. A teacher might say something like: "If you have something to say, share it with the whole class." Usually, this approach would temporarily put a halt to the murmuring, as verbally sharing with the class might not win new converts to their cause. Jesus had the opportunity to take action in a similar manner, but chose an alternate route.

The conversation among the Pharisees and teachers of the law was not directed at Jesus, but he was their focus. This group of spiritual leaders needed to get pumped up, before approaching Jesus in direct conversation. Jesus would give instruction on how to deal with adversity throughout his ministry on earth, and the approach of these leaders was in opposition to his teaching. Normally, listening to people muttering is like hearing indiscernible rhetoric. I picture it like listening to a small child trying to tell me where it hurts while sobbing, except that at least the child is trying to communicate to me. These people were murmuring behind Jesus' back. Yet, Jesus understood not only their conversation but also their heart.

Luke 15:2

*But the Pharisees and the teachers of the law **muttered**, "This man welcomes sinners and eats with them".*

There is a lot of insight here in the character of the religious leaders and the condition of their heart. Institutions are often crumbled, not by might, but by the words of a selected few behind the scene. Arrogance, pride, insecurity, and many other negative traits are often at the root. For a long time, the Pharisees were in high esteem in the religious world. They protected, interpreted, and enforced the law of God, as they knew it. They separated themselves from common people like some form of ceremonial cleansing process. Their haughty attitude demanded "I'm better than you" or "I can't associate with you". Their murmuring amongst themselves was like an ego pep talk to get support. Their strength was in their elite group.

We see the same thing in industry, politics, education, and even churches today. The theory of evolution from Charles Darwin was, and still is, just a theory, yet anyone who attempted to offer an opposing view was cast aside. The strength of the movement came from the meetings of those who accepted it as truth. Equally important was the desire to squelch any evidence that did not meet the theory's premises. The same can be said for those in other organizations who disagree with directives handed down from those holding authority statuses. Murmuring and complaining in front of those in leadership is usually a bad move. It is better to have open discussions with fellow believers in a common cause. In sports it is called "getting pumped up". The Pharisees in this account were in uncomfortable surroundings. Their curiosity meant that they had to observe Jesus, but the setting was not conducive to a spiritual pep rally, so they had to vent their thoughts somewhat subdued.

Jesus at a Pharisee's House

Speaking behind the back of someone with others can be referred to as gossip. Going to the person that you have a difference with is the first step in getting it resolved. Seeking out others, with the intent to get support for your opinions, does not solve anything. It shows cowardice and the need for an ego boost. These traits are not the ones used to build up an organization, especially not used in spreading the gospel of Christ. These leaders and teachers of the law had their own agenda and belief system, which did not coincide with what they were observing from the teachings of Jesus. Earlier in Luke we read of another encounter with the Pharisees, where Jesus went to the home of one and ate with him.

Luke 14: 1 – 14

1 One Sabbath, when Jesus went to eat in the house of a prominent Pharisee, he was being carefully watched.

2 There in front of him was a man suffering from dropsy.

3 Jesus asked the Pharisees and experts in the law, "Is it lawful to heal on the Sabbath or not?"

4 But they remained silent. So taking hold of the man, he healed him and sent him away.

5 Then he asked them, "If one of you has a son or an ox that falls into a well on the Sabbath day, will you not immediately pull him out?"

6 And they had nothing to say.

7 When he noticed how the guests picked the places of honor at the table, he told them this parable:

8 "When someone invites you to a wedding feast, do not take the place of honor, for a person more distinguished than you may have been invited.

9 If so, the host who invited both of you will come and say to you, 'Give this man your seat.' Then, humiliated, you will have to take the least important place.

10 But when you are invited, take the lowest place, so that when your host comes, he will say to you, 'Friend, move up to a better place.' Then you will be honored in the presence of all your fellow guests.

11 For everyone who exalts himself will be humbled, and he who humbles himself will be exalted."

12 Then Jesus said to his host, "When you give a luncheon or dinner, do not invite your friends, your brothers or relatives, or your rich neighbors; if you do, they may invite you back and so you will be repaid.

13 But when you give a banquet, invite the poor, the crippled, the lame, the blind,

14 and you will be blessed. Although they cannot repay you, you will be repaid at the resurrection of the righteous."

This account says that Jesus went to eat in the house of a "prominent Pharisee". This was not only one of the elite, but also one that was well known among them. This Pharisee may have thought that Jesus singled him out because of his stature in the religious community. He may have welcomed him as a friend, as well a teacher. He may have thought that this visit was to be expected. After all, shouldn't those entrusted with keeping the law be among the first to receive a visit from a comrade, and what a better time than on the Sabbath? But while Jesus was there he spoke about things that went against the present teaching.

Jesus answered the Pharisee's question with a question. He knew that a direct approach would stir the pot of dissension. The question from the Pharisee was tied to an interpretation of their law, concerning, healing on the Sabbath.

Jesus had insight into their motives for asking the question. He knew they were trying to trap him. Before he responded, however, it is interesting to note that Jesus healed the man on the Sabbath. Can you imagine the faces of the religious leaders on seeing that?

If he said it was unlawful to heal on the Sabbath, then they would have a case against Jesus as a lawbreaker, because he performed healing on the Sabbath. Jesus seemed to set himself up for a fall by purposefully performing a healing act before answering their question. If he said it was lawful, then they could cry heresy, as the laws that they interpreted were being willfully abused. Jesus chose the indirect answer. "If an ox fell into a pit, would it be lawful to save it?" The tables were turned. Now, any answer on their part could be used against them. They were silent.

This portion of the account has some amazing insights that we should not miss. The scene includes a downcast man with dropsy, a well-respected Pharisee, and eyes intent on every action Jesus would make. Jesus did not enter the picture with blinders on, but rather with purpose. He knew that he was about to be tested. He also knew how everything would end before his journey began on that day. Time is something reserved for mankind. God knew that man would sin from the beginning of Creation. He knew that Jesus needed to be sent to re-establish a blameless covenant between the Creation and the Creator. This was now the time to put that plan into reality. The Jewish leaders were protecting the very law that announced Jesus' coming, but they did not recognize who he was. Every atoning sacrifice, made by the priests up to that time, pointed to the ultimate one to be made on the Cross of Calvary.

Let's look at the discussion that follows in this account. First, Jesus knew that healing on the Sabbath was one area that went against the law at that time. So he went to the Pharisee's house on the Sabbath. He knew that he was being "carefully watched". He also knew his purpose was to "fulfill the law" not condemn it. All the laws stem from two, which are to love God and love your fellow man. A Pharisee asked Jesus what were the greatest commandments as we read in Matthew.

Matthew 22: 34-40

34 Hearing that Jesus had silenced the Sadducees, the Pharisees got together.

35 One of them, an expert in the law, tested him with this question:

36 "Teacher, which is the greatest commandment in the Law?"

37 Jesus replied: " 'Love the Lord your God with all your heart and with all your soul and with all your mind.'

38 This is the first and greatest commandment.

39 And the second is like it: 'Love your neighbor as yourself.'

40 All the Law and the Prophets hang on these two commandments."

Jesus had just met with the Sadducees regarding the question of marriage in heaven (verses 23 – 33). This group understood that heaven existed, but Jesus had firsthand information on the subject. He confronted them with a direct response. The Pharisees heard about the confrontation and rallied together. This account lets us know that one of them, an "expert in the law," raised the question to test Jesus. The implied intent was not to gain new insight or wisdom from his answer. Rather, the question was raised to find something to later use against him. Jesus knows our hearts before we ever utter a word from our mouths.

The guardians of the law had added scores of modifications. Many of these went directly against the two main ones. Healing on the Sabbath was a man-made law, and Jesus addressed it. First, Jesus healed a man of dropsy and then compared that with saving a son or ox that fell into a well. The Pharisee and his guests said nothing. Jesus knew how they would respond before performing the healing. He knew that act would trigger the question about healing on the Sabbath. This series of events was no accident.

Second, Jesus addressed their pride. The guests picked "places of honor" first, leaving lesser seats for those who came later. Once again, Jesus spoke to them using a parable. He addressed the concept of honor as how the host treats his guests, rather than how the guests choose their seating. At the same time Jesus spoke about who the guests should be. Rather than invite your closest friends, invite the poor, crippled, lame or blind. Then you will receive a blessing beyond earthly measure. Jesus had set the stage for why he was here, and he let the Pharisees know first-hand. The religious leaders murmured among themselves regarding the despicable association with sinners and tax collectors. Now Jesus is telling the leaders to invite the lowly and give them a place of honor. What a blow this must have been. Certainly the leaders would have reacted unfavorably.

One rotten apple can spoil a whole bushel. We have heard words like that in attempts to get unity in organizations. Rumors and innuendos need to be quickly squelched, or they begin to destroy societies. Left to fester they will infiltrate good organizations and begin to cause them to implode. They are like the oily rags starting to smolder and eventually becoming a blazing fire. The teachers and protectors of the law could not let go of their pride. They demanded respect. Jesus knew that the murmuring of this group of people needed to be dealt with.

Jesus also knew that those who accepted the false teachings needed to hear the truth. On one side we have the religious leaders needing answers to the things on their hearts. On the other side we have the everyday people who came to listen to the words of a welcomed stranger. These people probably had been indoctrinated with most of the ritualistic laws that covered spiritual growth. The insight of Jesus needed to be called upon to satisfy both groups and He chose to do that through parables. Those who received the wisdom of discernment would get it. Those who came with fixed motives would not.

We can think about the majesty of the solar system and everything in it, but knowing that the Creator also knows the number of hairs on our heads is even more amazing. The code, written on a single DNA molecule, contains a script for our lives that would take years to read if laid out from one end to the other. Yet, God read it before we were born. We visit a doctor to get wisdom and insight into what is the cause of the illness. We place our trust in someone with the training to get answers. We trust that a pilot will land the craft safely, since we are not qualified to fly a plane. Jesus had insight into everything that he would face, and now begins to put his Father's script into a finished work.

Questions to ponder:

☐ Can you identify a situation that you would have handled differently, if you had more insight upfront?

_____

☐ What usually happens when you act out of impulse without first gathering all the facts?

_____

☐ Have you ever taken great pains to understand an issue before addressing it? If so, what was the result?

_____

THE PSYCHOLOGY OF JESUS

Jesus had the advantage of knowing the hearts and minds of everyone who came in contact with him and also how to deal with each situation.

Woman caught in adultery

On another occasion the Pharisees and teachers of the law brought a woman caught in adultery and displayed her in front of Jesus. According to the law, she should be stoned to death, Jesus was teaching forgiveness and love. He used psychology to eliminate her accusers. Those who came to trap him into, either going against the law (stoning), or his new teaching (forgiveness and love), left without a single stone thrown.

John 8: 3-8

1 But Jesus went to the Mount of Olives.

2 At dawn he appeared again in the temple courts, where all the people gathered around him, and he sat down to teach them.

3 The teachers of the law and the Pharisees brought in a woman caught in adultery. They made her stand before the group

4 and said to Jesus, "Teacher, this woman was caught in the act of adultery.

5 In the Law Moses commanded us to stone such women. Now what do you say?"

6 They were using this question as a trap, in order to have a basis for accusing him. But Jesus bent down and started to write on the ground with his finger.

7 When they kept on questioning him, he straightened up and said to them, "If any one of you is without sin, let him be the first to throw a stone at her."

8 Again he stooped down and wrote on the ground.

Jesus was teaching in the temple courts. He sat down with everyone gathering around, much like we may do when reading story to children. It appeared to be a close fellowship, when the Jewish leaders came onto the scene with a woman caught committing adultery. Everyone would need to look up. We do not hear of any hesitation on their part when they defended their position, based on the Law of Moses. The woman was placed in front to the group for all to see. The people knew that adultery was a sin punished by stoning from this teaching. "Now what do you say?" was the question posed to Jesus.

Jesus "bent down" to write on the ground with his finger. Jesus was already sitting, so he, probably, leaned forward to reach the ground with his finger. I can picture the audience anxiously trying to see what Jesus was writing on the ground. I'm sure that the Jewish leaders had the same intent, and were, most likely, close enough to see every stroke. The account does not tell us anything about the writings, but during that time, the leaders kept on with their questions. Whatever Jesus was teaching before the entry of the leaders was quickly lost by the self-motivated actions of these leaders. "Answer us? Why are you turning away and writing on the ground?" may have been the gist of their taunts.

The first part of his psychology was to make them wait for his answer. He knew that might be uncomfortable for them. At the same time he knew they would probably think that they had him trapped for sure. He appeared to be writing in the sand. He knew exactly what he would say without the theatrics, but he also knew that a quick answer would not be as effective. Jesus also had a crowd around witnessing the event, with some level of curiosity in his response. He waited for the right time and simply told them to examine their own heart before hurling the first stone. No one felt righteous. One lesson we can learn from this is to not speak before thinking it through. That is why we have two eyes, two ears, and only one mouth. We are to use these senses in the same proportion; twice as much listening and observing before speaking.

Questions to ponder:

☐ The crowd observing Jesus may have been totally silent, waiting for Jesus to respond to the woman's accusers. What thoughts do you think they might have had during that moment of silence?

_____

☐ What thoughts can you imagine were in the minds of the accusers?

_____

☐ What do you think the woman was thinking about?

_____

☐ What significance can you see in the kneeling and writing in the sand?

_____

☐ Can you think of a time (or times) when you wish that you had taken a moment to gather your thoughts before speaking?

_____

The woman was the object of the question posed by these leaders, but Jesus was the one being judged. He let a moment of time pass before responding, to allow everyone to pause and think. The Jewish leaders may not have given much thought to anything, but their own agenda, namely, find fault with Jesus. The majority of those in the audience did not have preconceived ideas. Many of these people addressed their inner conscious. The verdict was rendered that the woman should receive punishment, based on the laws at that time. Yet, the one who could cast the first stone had to also be without sin. No one was without sin. Even the arrogance of the religious leaders was held at bay. They were pointing fingers at Jesus, and found even more pointing at them. A direct answer to their question, without the moment of silence, may have initiated the stoning. Jesus knew the outcome. After the woman's accusers turned away, we read these words:

John 8: 9-11

9 At this, those who heard began to go away one at a time, the older ones first, until only Jesus was left, with the woman still standing there.

10 Jesus straightened up and asked her, "Woman, where are they? Has no one condemned you?"

11 "No one, sir," she said. "Then neither do I condemn you," Jesus declared. "Go now and leave your life of sin."

One at a time the people left, starting with the oldest until Jesus was with the woman alone. Jesus taught the principle of repentance and forgiveness by his actions. It is interesting that the account tells us that the oldest left first. Leadership and wisdom may be synonymous with age. The younger people may have looked around to see how their elders reacted, before making their decision. Jesus must have been still kneeling in the sand while they left, as the account says that he "straightened up". What a picture! The one being accused of adultery was standing, while Jesus took the position of humility. Instead of looking down at the woman, she was looking down at Jesus. Jesus fully understood that adultery was wrong and should be punished. Yet, he pardoned her sin and gave the instruction to turn away from such behavior in the future.

Another interesting observation from this account is that it did not come as a surprise to Jesus. He taught from the Mount of Olives on the previous day and, purposely, went to the temple courts, where religious leadership would, certainly, be present. He was invading their territory. Therefore, it would only be natural to expect a confrontation. Word about Jesus teaching on the mountain, may well have gotten back to the members of the Sanhedrin, which led to the events in the temple.

Questions to ponder:

☐ The law required a public spectacle of stoning for the sin of adultery. What would be the motives for people to come, view and partake of such a punishment?

_____

☐ Do you think future stoning would inspire the same size crowd?

_____

☐ Many countries still have public displays like hanging. Do you think that deters criminal behavior?

_____

DENNIS A. MCINTYRE

THE STAGE IS SET

Luke chapter fifteen includes several parables, which Jesus shared with a crowd, including a familiar one referred to as "The Parable of the Prodigal Son." He had been teaching spiritual truths through parables, when the murmuring of the religious leaders began to become evident. Jesus knew what they were saying as well as their motivation. It was now time to address the disturbance with a new series of parables.

We read on another occasion that a woman, seeking to be healed, touched Jesus' cloak (Luke 8: 43 – 49). Though he was in a crowd of people, he felt her touch and said that her faith had healed her. When Lazarus died, he delayed several days before raising him up. He knew the hearts of those around. Perhaps, they would have doubted that Lazarus had actually died, if he was brought back to life soon afterwards, Jesus wanted there to be no doubt. He was dead. Jesus knew the hearts of the spiritual leaders stirring in the background as well as everyone else in his audience. The time has come to confront them, while at the same time, minister truths to all who would listen.

Jesus used different situations and circumstances to reveal truths. He knew that there was no single answer, which would apply to all conditions. Families realize this as well. Each of us has different languages that we respond to. For some it's a gentle touch. For others, words spoken in love can melt their hearts. Acts of love, gifts, and other areas can also speak volumes to those who are tuned in. We live in a society where we hope that a pill can cure everything. I know of no such pill for a broken heart.

Now we have the picture of these leaders and protectors of the law, arrogantly attempting to elevate themselves above everyone else, especially over Jesus. Jesus could have answered them with a straightforward and clear response, but it would have fallen on deaf ears. We have all contacted people who have their own agenda. They wait for you to stop speaking so they can get their point across. They get creative in trying other methods to be heard, but rarely hear themselves. Jesus heard their murmuring and knew that a direct answer to them would have been fruitless.

Then there is the matter of the crowd who would also hear the words of Jesus. If he took on the teachers with a direct response, not only would the teachers take exception, but also, many of those in the crowd. These people could have grown up with some form of respect for the Pharisees. They might well have reacted in defense. Jesus was the newcomer. Perhaps they came to hear what he had to say out of curiosity and had not yet formed an opinion of his character. Calling them a "Brood of vipers," as he did on another occasion, may have set off undesired results with the crowd.

If we put all of these things together, we can begin to see the incredible insights and wisdom of Jesus. He addressed the crowd with a series of parables. These were also intended for the Pharisees to hear without feeling that their pride was hurt. The messages were thoughtfully and systematically designed to penetrate all hearts, open to receive them. Those that weren't open to listen would miss out on the greatest opportunity of their lifetime.

Of the four Gospel writers Luke captures chronological details of the events that he witnessed. He was like a court stenographer, whose responsibility was to record the events so they could be read back on request. Luke named people, recorded parables and ensured the order of the events was true. Matthew, Mark and John wrote from different perspectives.

We are not programmed with the same tendencies. When a police investigation interviews multiple witnesses, each one sees the event differently. Suppose four vehicles witnessed a car accident from approximately the same distance away. A driver with a heart of service may totally overlook what caused the accident and focus on any injuries. The most important aspect would be the physical or emotional status of the passengers. Another driver with a teacher's heart may try to identify how the accident happened so that future ones could be avoided. Someone with the gift of prophecy may have approached the one who caused the accident with words like: "I knew that would happen by the way you sped by me." Each perspective, in itself, is not wrong. They are just different. The point is that four unique accounts have been recorded on the life and ministry of Jesus. Studying all four Gospels provides the most comprehensive understanding of Christ, His purpose and his teachings.

Questions to ponder?

☐ Do you tend to accept the first account that you receive about an issue, or do you seek further confirmation?

_____

☐ When accused of a crime, we can face a judge or a jury for a verdict. Why do you think our justice system was established with the right to trial by a jury of our peers?

_____

☐ Why do you think we have four Gospel accounts of the life of Jesus?

_____

DENNIS A. MCINTYRE

MATTHEW'S ACCOUNT

If I were to give a title to Matthew's account of Jesus' life it would be: "Good News". The Old Testament writings regarding a long-awaited Messiah were being fulfilled according to Matthew. As one of the twelve disciples Matthew captured Christ's teachings, miracles, and other events directly relating to Jesus as the promised one. Scholars believe that Matthew's account was probably written before the Romans destroyed the temple in Jerusalem in A.D. 70.

Matthew quotes the Old Testament scripture often and uses the phrase, "Kingdom of Heaven" just as frequently. Because of this it is widely believed that he was addressing the Jewish people. He presents Christ as the great teacher, who helps us understand God's law. Christ lets us know about a kingdom of God and what it is like. The "Sermon on the Mount" (5:1 – 7:27) is perhaps the most notable, but some of Christ's miracles and parables are also mentioned. Matthew uses Christ's teachings and miracles to emphasize that Jesus was the Son of God who triumphantly entered Jerusalem, died, was buried, and rose again. The book ends with the "Great Commission" of the eleven disciples to go into the entire world and make disciples. Jesus promises to never leave, even till the end of time. These words may well have inspired Matthew to let each of us today know this truth, as we become Disciples of Christ.

Matthew introduces a record of the genealogy of Jesus, demonstrating that he was from the lineage of David. Then we are given some details about Christ's birth that includes a virgin, angels and wise men. Each of these is directed towards the fulfillment of Old Testament prophecy. This was the "Good News" proclaimed to the world namely that the Messiah has come.

Questions to ponder:

☐ What events come to mind as recorded in the book of Matthew?

_____

☐ Do the words "I will never leave you or forsake you" give you any sense of peace?

_____

☐ Why do you think Jesus chose Matthew, Mark, Luke, and John to separately record the events of his time with them?

_____

MARK'S ACCOUNT

Mark was considered the first Gospel recorded. He focused on Facts, actions, themes, and topics. It is believed that Mark was the same person who worked for many years as a missionary with Paul and Barnabas. In Col. 4:10 we read of a man called Mark, who was the cousin of Barnabas.

Mark stresses actions and facts over themes or topics. His account begins with Isaiah's promise of a messenger who will prepare the way for the Lord and then lets us know that John the Baptist fulfilled this prophecy. Although Mark's account is the shortest of all the Gospels, it is filled with details. Jesus is depicted as a man of action and authority. Mark spends about one third of the time writing about Christ's last week of ministry.

Mark captures a few of the miracles performed by Jesus as well as some of Christ's parables. The "Parable of the Sower" (chapter 4) is given special attention to detail. Jesus spends time letting his audience know what each element of this parable represented, which Mark knew was crucial to spreading the Gospel of Jesus Christ. The importance of planting seeds is the responsibility of every believer independent of the soil available.

Jesus' triumphal entry into Jerusalem is described. Then Mark lets us know that Jesus went right to the temple, where he overturned the tables of the moneychangers. This account also fulfilled prophecy (Isa. 56:7 and Jer. 7:11). Mark concludes with Jesus' arrest, trial, crucifixion, death and resurrection. Like Matthew, Mark gives his version of the great commission (Mark 16:15 – 16).

Questions to ponder:

☐ How important are the facts in reaching a conclusion

_____

☐ How much can we learn from watching the actions of a person over his or her words?

_____

☐ Do you enjoy studying topics / themes over entire books in the Bible?

_____

JOHN'S ACCOUNT

John looks at the humanity of Jesus. His introduction seems to mirror the account in Genesis with the words, "In the beginning was the Word, and the Word was with God, and the Word was God". John let his readers know right up front that Jesus was there during creation of everything. Like Mark, John then introduces John the Baptist, who gives witness to Jesus as the promised Messiah. John wrote his account sometime between 90 and 100 A.D.

John included five miracles not mentioned in the other Gospels. Only two of the miracles recorded in the other Gospels are recorded in John. John includes no parables and stresses the relationships that Jesus had with individuals. Jesus is no longer a child, but a man on a mission. John is concerned about the last three years of Christ's life and presents Jesus' humanity as he reaches out to all who come to him with need. The signs and wonders recorded by John give testimony to the supernatural abilities of Jesus, proving that he is the Son of God. John also shows us that Jesus was totally human by recording times when he was tired, hungry, sad or loving.

John 3:16 is the most often quoted verse in the Bible; *"For God so loved the world, that he gave his one and only son, that whoever believes in him shall not perish, but have eternal life"*. These were the words of Jesus spoken to Nicodemus, who was a Pharisee and member of the Jewish ruling council (John 3:1). Jesus is teaching the Jewish teacher about eternal things. John records Christ's words so that we might also understand.

Like the other Gospels, John gives an account of Jesus' arrest, trial, crucifixion, death and resurrection. From this we can conclude that these points are essential to accept Christ as our personal savior.

Questions to ponder:

☐   How important is it to know that God came to earth and became fully human?

_____

☐   Do you think Jesus knows what you are going through because of His humanity

_____

☐   Why does John let His readers know up front the "The Word was with God" and "Was God?"

_____

LUKE'S ACCOUNT

The account of the prodigal son in Luke is the focus in this book. The writings of Luke give us a detailed order that can be studied to gain insights into the heart of Jesus, as he presented the parable. Luke begins chapter 15 with Jesus addressing a crowd of people considered to be outcasts in society with the religious leaders murmuring in the background. Through all of the noise, Jesus not only knew what they were muttering, but also their hearts. The rest of this book will delve into his response. Perhaps we can learn something about how to deal with difficult people or gain new insights into the character of Jesus Christ.

Luke was a doctor. Matters of the heart may have been part of his bedside manner to his patients. Medicine could only go so far. Some cures could only come through internal change. As a doctor, the order, in which events took place, may be significant in a diagnosis. Therefore, Luke starts this series of parables by recognizing the distraction caused by the Jewish leaders. Those living by train tracks, often, do not hear the trains pass. Their minds, somehow, ignore the sounds after time. Wives may accuse their husbands of similar tactics, when asked to perform a chore. In this account, however, Luke lets us know that Jesus could hear the muttering amongst the Pharisees and teachers of the law. He also lets us know that the parables, that would follow, were directly related to the leaders.

Questions to ponder:

☐ What areas are common in all four Gospels?

_____

☐ Do these accounts offer unique insights into the character of Jesus or His message?

_____

THE PARABLE OF THE LOST SHEEP

Jesus began his reply with the story of 100 sheep, where one was lost.

Luke 15: 3 – 7

3 Then Jesus told them this parable:

4 "Suppose one of you has a hundred sheep and loses one of them. Does he not leave the ninety-nine in the open country and go after the lost sheep until he finds it?

5 And when he finds it, he joyfully puts it on his shoulders

6 and goes home. Then he calls his friends and neighbors together and says, 'Rejoice with me; I have found my lost sheep.'

7 I tell you that in the same way there will be more rejoicing in heaven over one sinner who repents than over ninety-nine righteous persons who do not need to repent.

"Suppose one of you…" is an interesting way of drawing an audience into what the speaker has to get across to them. The movie "A Time to Kill" involved an African-American father who took the lives of two men who raped, beat, and left his daughter for dead. The attorney, who defended him, made a closing argument that had the jury close their eyes. He told the jury a detailed account of the daughter's peril. The scene was in a southern town in segregated America. The panel of twelve had already placed a guilty verdict on their minds. None of them were black and bigotry was their mindset. Then the defense attorney, with their eyes closed, told them to picture the daughter's beaten, bloody and defamed body. "Can you see her?" he cried. He repeated those words again with more clarity. Then he told them to picture that little girl "White. His argument was to get them to see without bigotry or bias. The verdict was a unified "not guilty". "Suppose" is a powerful word.

Then Jesus said "*One of you*". There was an audience of people there and yet each one was treated as an individual. Each one would have to judge individually, as to how they would interpret his words. The parable would have a worldly application with the focus on a sheep, yet the one in charge had to deal with finding the lost sheep. Jesus placed the concept of ownership on each person there. Not only did they have to understand the concept of one lost sheep, but also they needed to understand the concept of shepherding. Jesus asked the members of His audience to put themselves in the mindset of a shepherd as they listened to the parable. Many of those who listened would not have a problem, as that was their livelihood. This would be more difficult for the religious leadership.

I remember attending a session by Stephen Covey on his book "First Things First", which was one of his habits related to a character trait of highly effective people. The site was a large ballroom inside a sizeable hotel. To get to the room was like walking in a maze. We took our seats at round tables with eight chairs around each. I share this because Dr Covey began his message by telling us to close our eyes. He told us that the person, facing north at each table, would be responsible to teach the others on each point made in the seminar. Then he asked for the raising of hands by anyone who was facing north. By the time I sat down I couldn't tell which direction the front door of the hotel faced, let alone which way is north in the room. Nevertheless, I raised my hand, as did about seventy-five percent of those there. His point was that if we felt that we had to pass on the information, we would pay closer attention to what was said. I erred on the caution side, in case my chair actually faced north. Jesus said, "Suppose one of you". Perhaps each in attendance felt that person was them. Would they listen with a similar intensity?

Sheep are considered dumb animals. They can easily wander and lose their way. They would follow other sheep blindly, even off a cliff. Shepherds of that day knew this all too well. We don't know how many of those listening were shepherds, but we can assume that the duties of a shepherd were widely known. To the Pharisees shepherds would have been on the bottom of the economic chain. To associate with a shepherd might be a rare photographic moment today. Yet, those who tended the sheep would have related to the story. They would have searched high and low for the one that was lost, leaving the ninety-nine. The ninety-nine had each other, but one was lost and needs to be rescued before falling prey to other animals.

Sheep were also recognized for another very important service, that the Pharisees were well aware of, namely for ritual sacrifice according to Jewish law. Jesus himself made the ultimate sacrifice, when he died for his creation. John the Baptist called Jesus "The Lamb of God, who takes away the sins of the world" (John 1:29). These were prophetic words, as Jesus had just started his ministry. Atonement for sin according to the Old Testament law required a blood sacrifice, and a lamb was the standard choice. In Genesis 22:13, a ram (male sheep) was provided for a sacrifice, after God tested Abraham's faith by asking him to sacrifice his son Isaac. Sheep were an important symbol for their owners. Shepherds were rarely landowners, nor were the sheep cared for on their own. Perhaps Jesus was using this parable to prick the spiritual hearts of the religious leaders in a subconscious way.

Jesus questions the group, *"Does he not leave the ninety-nine in the open country and go after the lost sheep until he finds it?* We can picture the open country as a plain, where bushes and trees did not obstruct the view. Shepherds can see long distances and spot potential intruders in time to take protective action on behalf of the sheep. The areas filled with cover would have been an ideal location for the lost sheep to fall prey. The question demanded the answer "Of course he would leave and search." Remember, Jesus placed the symbolic burden of the shepherd on each person there, since each one would have considered him or her as being the "one." Rhetorical questions are another common technique to stir people and imaginations.

Can you picture something in your life that demanded for you to drop everything for a new purpose, and do it until completed? Such a task is not taken lightly. We would need single-mindedness, dedication, and the resolve to see it through. Jesus was asking them to get focused. They needed to know something about priorities. Then Jesus changed the story to reflect a deeper fundamental truth, one that took them away from the physical realm. Suddenly heaven is rejoicing over the one lost sheep that is now safely returned to the fold. The "One" who found it was so overjoyed, that everyone needed to share his joy with him. Anyone with children has experienced that kind of joy, when their child accomplished the smallest task. The parent would proudly pick the child up, and then parade through a crowd to let everyone know the joy he or she was feeling. Heaven shares a great joy when even one lost soul returns.

What a picture. One group came to hear what Jesus had to share with them. The other sought to undermine Jesus, as they saw him as a threat. One sought to improve their status, while the other desired to maintain it. One was searching for answers about heavenly things, and the other was clinging to their earthly power. Jesus not only had to address them both, but do it in a manner that would not come across offensively. He had to speak to their minds in order to penetrate their hearts. Surely, the story of sheep would not raise any dander, yet Jesus used it to begin the heart massage process. Great joy permeates from the heart. It leaps out without forethoughts. To solicit that kind of response using words, demonstrates a deep knowledge of the human spirit. Jesus knew their hearts. He desired to have all of them come to know him and receive the unspeakable joy only he could offer.

Have you ever observed a psychologist at work? Patients may be off the wall with their emotions, but the doctor is low keyed and calm. Words are used as catalysts to get the patient to respond from their suppressed emotions. The role of the psychologist is to get the patient to recognize their problems and make decisions to change direction that would provide the needed relief. The healing process came from within. The role of the doctor was simply to get the emotional barriers and struggles to come to the forefront, where they can be resolved. That was the role Jesus was playing here. Each person would have to hear his message and decide what it meant to him or her personally. Jesus was speaking to a crowd one person at a time.

Let me remind you that the Pharisees listened as they murmured. Perhaps, they didn't even know that the story was not only for them, but also about them. They did not come out and formally ask Jesus any questions. Their murmuring was about why Jesus was with "tax collectors and sinners". Perhaps, their first thoughts were "what do sheep have to do with these people?" They could have thought that sheep and shepherding were low on the chain of significance, like those attending. This story may have been interesting, but certainly not directed at them.

The message Jesus had was about turning from sin. The Jewish leaders considered "sinners" as a group outside of their social group. Therefore, repentance was something that these people needed to come to them to receive. Jesus added a subtle comment, which seems to be pointed directly at the Jewish leaders. He spoke about the ninety-nine "righteous persons" who don't need to repent. These leaders considered themselves as righteous.

Questions to ponder:

☐ What do you think of, when you think of sheep? …shepherds?

_____

☐ Have you ever felt relief or joy when you found something lost?

_____

☐   When you felt an occasion of true elation, how did it affect those around you?

_____

☐   How quickly were you willing to share your new joy?

_____

THE PARABLE OF THE LOST COIN

After first sharing the parable of the one lost sheep out of a hundred, Jesus then switched to an inanimate object, namely a coin. This time we are to consider one coin out of ten. The Pharisees may well have felt the first story as being insignificant. "One sheep out of a hundred, why bother" may have permeated their thoughts. Now Jesus uses a silver coin. Silver would have had more significance to them. It was a symbol of their elite status. Yet, even with this parable, Jesus uses another character to bring things down to earth. He introduces a woman. Tax collectors and shepherds were one thing, but women were even lower on the social status chain. We don't know how many women were in the audience. We can only imagine that some were there. The women may not have related as well to the parable of the lost sheep, but losing a silver coin would have been a different story. Wealth was rarely attributed to Jewish women.

Luke 15: 8 – 10

8 *"Or suppose a woman has ten silver coins and loses one. Does she not light a lamp, sweep the house and search carefully until she finds it?*

9 And when she finds it, she calls her friends and neighbors together and says, 'Rejoice with me; I have found my lost coin.'

10 In the same way, I tell you, there is rejoicing in the presence of the angels of God over one sinner who repents."

Jesus said, "**Suppose a woman**". Again we are to suppose something, but this time the picture has a woman with ten silver coins. The value of silver was not as high as gold, yet to a woman it was a valued treasure. Perhaps, it represented a long period of scrimping and saving. To replace even a single coin would take weeks or even months. Perhaps it represented a wedding gift that took on special significance, much like a wedding ring. We are not told of where the coins came from. Rather we are told that they carried great significance to the owner, who would not give up until the lost coin was found.

Can you remember working hard to earn money to purchase something that you really wanted? It may have been your first car, a new sound system, or a wedding band. Once you had the money to buy it, you guarded it with your life. The panic you may have felt when the item was damaged in some way, like a scratch on the car's paint, would have set you off to get it repaired. What if you finally had the money only to have part of it missing? The item was almost in you hands, and suddenly, you would have to wait. When we go through times like these, we can easily relate to the woman in this story much like Jesus' audience.

We can only imagine what the teachers of the law were thinking. Women were also not held very high in their world, but money had value. It was only one coin out of ten. She would still have nine. Possessions were status to these leaders. Replacing a single coin would have been relatively quick, so spending a lot of time searching for the one lost coin may have sounded trivial. Nevertheless, it was something of value, that they may have perked up their ears to hear more of the words of Jesus.

She left no stone unturned. She searched everywhere using all of the resources at hand. She used a lamp so that the dark corners of her home were not hidden to her. She sifted through the floor sweepings. Jesus said she did this carefully. She was not to be denied. Her tenacity would have been her greatest asset. With that kind of attitude, how much joy could she have felt when the coin was found. The relief must have been tremendous. Her joy was so great that she called her friends and neighbors to share her excitement with her.

Who do we call when we are that full of utter joy? In the summer of 1999 I went down to spend time with my dad, who was finishing his years in a nursing home in Florida. At the age of eighty-seven, he had a stroke. Most of his abilities were lost or severely hampered, but he still had his mind. I desired to lead him to a saving knowledge of my Lord and Savior, Jesus Christ. His wife (our mother) took Christ as her savior when I was a baby and then died soon afterwards. Dad had a Christian upbringing, but her death turned him away. He blamed God for her death and sought peace in life through his three sons, along with his extra activities. He was a life master bridge player, avid stamp collector, reader, puzzle solver, and much more. He would not let himself have a moment, where he would have to hear the wee small voice of God calling him. Yet, now all those things were lost. "How could God take his wife after she accepted Jesus as he Savior?" That question caused my dad to reject the loving God, he knew from his youth. I made regular visits for fourteen months to the nursing home. I shared Christ with him, but felt the bitterness. If I could get him to laugh, then somehow the visit would have been considered a success.

Then one day in October of 2000, I decided to be baptized by emersion. It meant that I would have to cut my visit short with dad. I shared that with him over our typical late breakfast at his favorite restaurant in the area. During one of my earlier visits I gave him a giant print Bible, with the hopes that he could see well enough to read some of it. On this day the Bible was in his wheel chair. When I helped him into the van and loaded the chair, I also placed the Bible into his lap. Then I got into the driver's seat. I asked him whether he was reading the Bible. He said, "I try". Then I asked him if he had questions that I might be able to answer. His response blew me away. He said, "All I know is that I want to go to heaven, because I think that is where my boys are going to be". My heart leaped for joy. Before I left on that day, my dad accepted the Lord as his personal savior.

I drove back to be baptized with a heart that was so full of joy that I had to share it with everyone, starting with my wife. She was in New York, but thank God for cell phones. I don't think I said more than a few words, but the tears in my voice still got the message home. Then I called my oldest brother, who also was trying to reach dad for the kingdom. Again the tears spoke far more than any words. Finding one silver coin may not have been as great as knowing that my dad was now spared an eternal death, but I can relate nonetheless. "Rejoice with me" were her words, just as they were mine on that day. That giant print Bible has one page listed with my name for being baptized and dad's name for being saved. It will forever be a reminder to me of the joy that I felt that day.

Verse ten then tells us *"In the same way, I tell you, there is rejoicing in the presence of the angels of God over one sinner who repents."* Jesus used a woman and a coin to get this message across once more. My wife rejoiced with me, as did my brother. But, here he tells us that even heaven rejoiced with the angels. The illustration of a silver coin is compared with a lost sinner. The act of finding the coin is synonymous to repentance. Sheep were used as a sin offering. They were considered dumb animals, and stupidity was not a sin. The parable of the lost coin uses an inanimate object, which has no association with sin. Then, Jesus makes a comparison to a lost sinner. Just like the woman rejoices, when she finds the coin, so does heaven rejoice when a lost sinner is found. In the case of a sinner, however, recognizing sin needs to be accomplished by the one sinning. The act of repentance requires turning away from sin. The religious leaders needed to recognize their self-centered arrogance and selfish ambitions were sin.

What a picture for the believer. Those in the audience may not have had the experience like I had in the story about my dad's salvation. They would have to somehow understand Jesus' teaching. Perhaps many did, but what about the Pharisees?

The psychology of Jesus continues. We can imagine the murmuring slowing to a whisper or more directed at the meaning of the parables. The sequence from one lost sheep in a hundred has progressed to one coin in ten. It is like placing a slide on a microscope and focusing in on the details. Things start out looking fuzzy, but as the scope is adjusted the clarity improves. At this point the image is still not sharp, but the edges are showing more definition. Jesus has carefully and methodically made the first adjustment. The clarity of the image will now depend on the cleanliness of the lenses used, namely the hearts of those listening. Ultimately, Jesus knew the hearts of the Pharisees where we can see the microscope adjustment moving.

Questions to ponder:

☐ Have you ever searched for something and not found it?

_____

☐ What feelings did you experience in the process of searching?

_____

☐ Is there anytime in your life when you felt God had abandoned you or did not exist?

_____

☐ Can you share an account in your life that proved to you that God does exist?

_____

Dennis A. McIntyre

THE WAYWARD SON

The focus has now been adjusted to the very heart of his message. Jesus softened their hearts to now be ready to hear the part that he desired from the beginning. He knew that to share this parable first would not only have come on deaf ears, but it's meaning would almost certainly be missed. Dealing with arrogant, stubborn, selfish, or self-centered people is like talking to a wall. Words bounce off rather than penetrate. We can all take a lesson from the manner, in which Jesus handled the murmuring teachers.

Bull in a china shop

As an electrical engineer, I always desired to perform my responsibilities the best that I could. Staying on time and below the budget were strong motivational goals as well. Roadblocks, which would delay a project, would serve as opportunities for me to overcome, through creative planning. I was the bull in the china shop, when it came to staying the course. Whenever people would hinder the progress that I intended, I would fight back all the more. Not only would this not improve the work, but also, it would often alienate the workers.

One day another engineer came and shared my bullish tendencies to me. He told me that trying to break down a wall by force can have only two outcomes, and neither would solve the problem. First, I would only cause pain to myself, and the wall stays firm. Second, I would suddenly cause the wall to disintegrate, and everyone on the other side would point fingers saying that I was the one caused it to fall. In neither case, no one would see what was on the other side of the wall, as I intended. Then he handed a spoon to me and said, "Use this." I told him to give me a sledgehammer. He said, "You don't get it. Use the spoon." I asked him how and he replied, "Chip away at the mortar a little bit at a time. Then the wall will fall without anyone knowing how, and they will see what is on the other side."

Jesus used this principle by telling the first two parables, before getting to where the wall could fall without too much more help. By the end of the story of the lost coin, the mortar was cracked and weak. The Pharisees may have stopped the murmuring, to see where these parables were going. Curiosity may have replaced animosity. Now we can watch psychology in action as Jesus lowers the gauntlet and brings his message to conclusion.

Luke 15: 11 – 13

11 Jesus continued: "There was a man who had two sons.

12 The younger one said to his father, 'Father, give me my share of the estate.' So he divided his property between them.

13 "Not long after that, the younger son got together all he had, set off for a distant country and there squandered his wealth in wild living.

In this account Jesus does not ask them to "suppose" they were someone else. He continues directly into the story of a father with two sons. Perhaps this was a picture, which all could relate and common to many of the men there. He spoke about an ordinary occurrence, as it was normal for sons to be heirs of a father's estate. Normally an heir receives his inheritance upon the father's death or near the end of his life. Here, one son decides not to wait. He was impetuous and asks for it sooner. We can theorize all sorts of reasons for his request, but as we will see, he no longer desired to follow in his family's footsteps.

We are also told that it was the younger son who made the request. I grew up with two other brothers, each about a year apart in age. My older brother had the leadership role, while my younger brother seemed to be more of the party-goer. People tend to seek out their own identity in life. We see it in different personalities. We also see it in the friends that we keep. The younger son seemed to be doing just that in the story. He decided that the grass would be greener in another place. He needed money to go there and boldly asked his father for his inheritance.

Family relationships can be extremely influential in shaping our character. We are not told about any acts of favoritism exhibited by the father towards the eldest son. Both sons had work to do. We could theorize, that the work being accomplished by the oldest son may have appeared more significant than the accomplishments of the youngest. Each of my brothers developed different character traits due, primarily, by birth order. My older brother focused on high grades and schoolwork. As the middle brother, I threw my schoolwork on the bed and went to work. If the local farmers did not have work for me to do, then you might see me helping dad in the yard. My younger brother hung with school friends. We were brothers but not clones. Our personalities differed, but we stilled honored our father who did not show favoritism. We may have chosen different paths, but we did not rebel against our father. Some of Jesus' listeners may have pictured the youngest son's action as rebellion or a break from traditional values.

Then we have another character in the story; the father. Those of you who have children, how would you respond? As a father I would allow my children to explore many new things, but it would be foolish for me to take half of what I owned and give it away, without knowing where it would be used. Many of us may have felt we did just that, during the years of college payments or music lessons. We make investments in our children to help them find their way in life, but at least we kept our other assets. I cannot picture a Pharisee in that day parting with half of anything, especially for the younger son. I can visualize their ears perking, however, over the fact that Jesus uses earthly wealth to make his point. From the account we understand that the father divided his property and gave the younger son his due.

What does that say about the father? He honored his son's wishes and let him go off with the fruit of his labors. He may have thought that he would never see him again, yet he let him leave anyway. I can sense the sadness that he must have felt, as he watched his son disappear in the horizon. The son needed to find his own way. The father knew that he could not make the choices for his son. He had to let him go. Parents let go of their children, when they leave to go to college or marry. They would no longer have the comforts of home, but they would take with them the love of a father. In this story love would also bring the young son back.

Questions to ponder:

☐ Place yourself in the shoes of the eldest son. What might be your reaction in seeing your brother take his inheritance while the father was still living?

_____

☐ If you were the youngest son, how would you feel towards your father for honoring your wishes?

_____

☐ What might be your thoughts as the father, when the request is made?

_____

Other differences between the first two parables and this one become evident. The coin and the sheep were somehow lost without any explanation. Three players are now mentioned, namely, the father and his two sons. A son is leaving, and both the father and his brother accepted it. They did not have to search for him. They accepted the fact that the son was leaving voluntarily. In the next part of the parable we see the result of his decision.

Luke 15: 14 – 20

13 *"Not long after that, the younger son got together all he had, set off for a distant country and there squandered his wealth in wild living.*

14 *After he had spent everything, there was a severe famine in that whole country, and he began to be in need.*

15 *So he went and hired himself out to a citizen of that country, who sent him to his fields to feed pigs.*

16 *He longed to fill his stomach with the pods that the pigs were eating, but no one gave him anything.*

17 *"When he came to his senses, he said, 'How many of my father's hired men have food to spare, and here I am starving to death!*

18 *I will set out and go back to my father and say to him: Father, I have sinned against heaven and against you.*

19 *I am no longer worthy to be called your son; make me like one of your hired men.'*

20 *So he got up and went to his father.*

He took everything with him, indicating, that the likelihood of his return was slim or none. Making that even clearer, Jesus states that he went to another country. Travel from one town to another in those times would have been a day, two, or even more. With automobiles and airplanes today, we see a trip to another country in hours. The idea that he went to a nearby town might indicate a temporary separation was possible. Jesus lets his listeners know that this son left the country. The likelihood of never returning was a real possibility.

The story continues by letting us know that he squandered all his wealth. This implies that the son had not learned the concepts of stewardship. In a short time, what took the father a long time to build up was foolishly spent. Whatever caused the son to ask for his inheritance appears to be deep-seated. The act of squandering implies recklessness. The son seemed to act impulsively. There did not appear to be a game plan. He took the money and ran as far away from his Father as he could. He spelled "relief" with each wasteful purchase. We can only imagine how the money was spent, but because of the son's regret, it wasn't spent wisely. It was as if the son was so upset about his life, that he was willing to make a complete turnaround. Hard work on the family's land, turned into a quest for pleasure and self-gratification.

I remember listening to a sermon one Easter morning, involving the thief called Barabbas. Three thieves were to be crucified on Calvary that day, but the angry crowd chose Jesus to take the place of the worst one, named Barabbas. I knew about this account from numerous sermons and studies in the past, but this message offered a new twist. The term "Bar" meant "Son of." Jesus would have been known as "Jesus Bar Joseph," for example. "Abbas" meant "priest." The minister concluded that the worst criminal that day had a name that implied "Son of a priest." To go from a priest's son to a criminal would take a complete turnaround. That story came to my mind, as I tried to envision the motives behind the youngest son's desires.

Then Jesus speaks of a severe famine in that country. Perhaps many of his listeners could relate to famine as a time when food was scarce. Even those who had money might find it difficult to acquire the basics they needed, but without money the concepts would have been bleak. Famine was a way to add emphasis to the desperation that this son must have been going through. It was one thing to squander all of you money and have to search for ways to earn more, but even with money, food was scarce. Pains of hunger can be a strong motivator to re-evaluate your position. The famine placed the added emphasis that this wayward son was in a very deep hole.

I have visited a few prisons as part of a ministry to the inmates. Prison is a place where feelings of despair and hopelessness are normal. It can be like looking up from a deep pit without hope. Yet, it was also in that place where I witnessed the dynamics of joy and peace in inmates who changed their lives, and accepted Christ as their Lord and Savior. These people would have made the average church attendee look like they were the ones imprisoned. Often, when we reach our lowest point, we finally get our act together and realize that we made a mess of things. Our decisions proved to be the wrong ones. This son was in that place.

Jesus says, **"When he came to his senses"**. Have you ever noticed how parents suddenly lose all of their intelligence when their children become teenagers, only to gain it all back just as suddenly when the children mature in adulthood? The bumper sticker with the words "Hire a teenage while they still know it all" sums it up nicely. Life involves choices, and unfortunately, those who make them must also deal with their consequences. The wayward son was so low that he even desired the slop of pigs. What a picture of despair. No one gave him anything. His stomach must have been growling so loud that it could be heard for miles.

Then he turned back to the last area where he felt loved, accepted, and oh yes, full. Even his father's hired hands are treated with more respect. His heart ached for even that level of satisfaction. He decided to return and become a worker, instead of having the privileges of a son. He no longer felt worthy to be called a son. He took everything that was due him as his inheritance, which may have severed any family ties, at least in his mind. Life, as a hired hand on his father's farm, was suddenly much more appealing than the life he was living, or should we say existing. The grass that looked so much greener when he left was now brown and ugly. A bed of straw with the animals was now a welcomed sight.

Questions to ponder:

☐ Have you ever had times when things looked bleak?

_____

☐ How did you handle those times?

_____

☐ If you suddenly lost all of your earthy values, where would you turn?

_____

☐ After recovering from feelings of despair, what did you value?

_____

Then we see another difference between the first two parables and this one. Not only did the son decide to return, but also he purposed to right the wrong that he perceived between him and his father. He said; *"Father, I have sinned against heaven and against you. I am no longer worthy to be called your son; make me like one of your hired men."* Not only did he recognize his shortcoming with his father, but also with God ("against heaven"). Jesus was now drawing everything together for those listening, especially for the teachers of the law.

Sin separates us from God. Adam and Eve learned this lesson. Through their seeds, sin entered the world. Atonement needed to be made to restore the relationship. The Jewish leaders knew about the sacrificial acts, which were required. Jesus let His audience know that first, the son needed to come to his senses and recognize what he had done. The religious leaders needed to do the same thing. They were zealous in defending their righteousness. When we take a good look back at the events and decisions that caused us to stray from the path God desires for us, then we can begin to get insights on how to get on the right path.

Second, once everything was evaluated, a new direction needed to be taken. When we get to the edge of a cliff, the choices get pretty simple. Either we continue to our destruction, or we turn around. The meaning of repentance is to "turn around." This son evaluated all that he had done, and recognized that he had made some bad decisions. God's gift of "free will" allows each of us to make decisions. God is not in the business of making decisions for us. We are not puppets. We own our choices. We also own the consequences of our decisions. The realization of this son that he sinned against his father was the first step to the healing process.

Third, the son knew that he had to return to his father and ask for forgiveness. He envisioned that he would have to work for his livelihood as a hired hand. His sin against his father was so great that heaven was affected. He turned from his earthly father when he left, with everything due to him in an inheritance. The son adds the perspective that he also grieved his heavenly Father. The son might feel forgiven if his father would take him in as a hired hand. He felt unworthy of anything more. The thoughts and feelings, that he had when he left, were now turned to pleasing his father and God. He needed to live a changed life of faith in something beyond himself. He did not know what to expect when he returned, but he knew that he had to go back.

Two principles are at work here. First, when we sense that we have wronged someone, we need to acknowledge that we did just that. This is our act of repentance. We become humble and genuinely sorrowful for our actions. Second, we seek forgiveness for our actions. This son admitted that he sinned against his father, and he was no longer worthy to be even called his son. Once we are a parent, we are always a parent. The same is true for son-ship. We may not feel as though we earned that right, but we are sons or daughters by all legal and ethical interpretations. Knowing that we are forgiven helps us to ease the emotions that hold us hostage.

The concept of admitting when we are wrong was a relatively new one to the Pharisees. When Jesus challenged the Pharisee (Luke 14) regarding healing on the Sabbath, he did not answer. That would be admitting that Jesus disobeyed the law, to not heal on the Sabbath. That was a day to be kept holy. Somehow, performing healing on the Sabbath, when the day was set aside for worship, was a sin. Yet they did not answer Jesus. Certainly, they would have saved an animal that had fallen in a well, no matter what day it was as Jesus suggested.

Coming to the conclusion that we have wronged someone, as the wayward son did, requires a humble spirit. Humility was another quality that these teachers of the law lacked. Their heads were so high in the clouds, that nosebleeds would have been more common than any utterance of sorrow. There are cultures in this world that seem to teach their men the concept, that it is a sign of weakness to admit you are wrong. It seems as though these cultures teach them to always turn the conversation around so that either, blame is placed elsewhere, or the subject is dropped. Have you ever known people like that? Humility is a virtue to God. It delves deep into the soul of a person. It comes from the heart. The Pharisees needed a heart transplant as far as Jesus was concerned.

The concept of repentance is another mystery of God. Not only, are we to become humble and admit our wrongdoings, but also we are to turn away from the behavior that caused the problem. It is not enough to understand that we failed, but to learn to not repeat the offence in the future. The wayward son learned that lesson, when he told his father he sinned against him. He humbled himself, and returned to the point, where he was taught right from wrong. He knew he did wrong, and desired to stop that behavior. The Pharisees had a much harder time to understand what it means to repent since they first needed to grasp the concept of humility.

That leads to the third concept of forgiveness. As far as God is concerned, without humility and a repentant spirit, we cannot receive forgiveness. The first two concepts lead us to ask for it. Forgiveness is a form of healing to the human spirit. If we wronged another and felt a genuine sorrow, the sadness can consume us. We could tell ourselves that we are worthless. We could hold ourselves slaves to the offence, or seek reconciliation from the one offended. The act of asking for forgiveness is something that touches the heart of God. Receiving forgiveness lifts veils of sorrow and adds unspeakable joy.

The wayward son returned home humble, repentant, and sought forgiveness. The father saw him a way off and, without hesitation, was prepared to celebrate.

Luke 15:20 -21

20 "But while he was still a long way off, his father saw him and was filled with compassion for him; he ran to his son, threw his arms around him and kissed him.

21 "The son said to him, 'Father, I have sinned against heaven and against you. I am no longer worthy to be called your son.

The father was filled with compassion for his son. Seeing him return even a long way off was a heart pounding experience. That moment, probably, brought tears of joy. This son left with all his possessions to go to a foreign country. As far as this father was concerned, he might never see him again, yet there he was. Without words being spoken the father ran to his son, hugged him, and kissed him. Can you imagine how the son must have felt? He was coming with a sorrowful heart, and was greeted by his father with shear joy and love. He may have thought he was so unworthy of being treated that way. Can you picture the father running towards him? I don't recall any time in my adult life when I saw my father running to me. His arms may have been open wide, while the son ran towards him. But, this father ran to be with his lost son. The joy must have been indescribable. The son did not need words to recognize that the father welcomed him home. We can only imagine the relief and joy in his heart as well.

The son opened his heart to the father. He admitted his shortcomings and demonstrated humility. **"I am no longer worthy to be called your son."** He had just been kissed and hugged by his father and felt unworthy. He was returning to work as a hired hand, and such a position would have been uplifting in itself. Yet, like the lost sheep and the lost coin, he had returned. What was once lost has been found. The father's joy was unspeakable. Jesus wanted the Pharisees and teachers of the law to understand these principles, and that would take a change of their heart.

Questions to ponder:

☐ Can you recall an event that made a significant difference in your spiritual journey?

_____

☐ Have you ever had a time of reconciliation with your parents? (If so discuss how you felt)

_____

☐ Have you ever felt unworthy in a relationship?

_____

☐ Are you experiencing guilt or shame involving your relationship with a family member or friend today?

_____

WHO WAS THE WAYWARD SON?

Most sermons on the parable of the prodigal (wayward) son focused on the son who took his inheritance, squandered it, and returned with a repentant heart. But was that what Jesus was trying to teach them? This account has significant differences from the first two parables of sheep and coins. We see the concepts of humility and repentance now added, but then there's more.

Luke 15: 22 – 31

22 "But the father said to his servants, 'Quick! Bring the best robe and put it on him. Put a ring on his finger and sandals on his feet.

23 Bring the fattened calf and kill it. Let's have a feast and celebrate.

24 For this son of mine was dead and is alive again; he was lost and is found.' So they began to celebrate.

25 "Meanwhile, the older son was in the field. When he came near the house, he heard music and dancing.

26 So he called one of the servants and asked him what was going on.

27 'Your brother has come,' he replied, 'and your father has killed the fattened calf because he has him back safe and sound.'

28 "The older brother became angry and refused to go in. So his father went out and pleaded with him.

29 But he answered his father, 'Look! All these years I've been slaving for you and never disobeyed your orders. Yet you never gave me even a young goat so I could celebrate with my friends.

30 But when this son of yours who has squandered your property with prostitutes comes home, you kill the fattened calf for him!'

31 " 'My son,' the father said, 'you are always with me, and everything I have is yours.

32 But we had to celebrate and be glad, because this brother of yours was dead and is alive again; he was lost and is found.' "

Like the other parables, there is great celebration for the return of the lost son. This time the father demonstrated his joy, by placing the finest robe on the son who returned. Then he ordered the best (fattened) calf to be killed for a great feast. His son was dead and is alive again. He was lost and now found. The celebration began.

The other son heard the excitement, when he finished his duties in the field and neared the house. So he called one of his servants to see what was going on. When Jesus began telling these parables, the Pharisees and teachers of the law were murmuring about what Jesus was doing with sinners. Jesus is now using the other son to show the same thing. This son did not go in and ask the father. Rather he consulted with one of his fellow workers. The news of his father's actions on behalf of his brother was disturbing to say the least. He became angry, and would not enter his house.

The father must have known that his eldest son was outside and had refused to come in, as he went out to urge him to share in his happiness. He pleaded with his son to help him understand, but the son's anger was too great. The son began his defense with justification. He did everything that the father had asked of him, and yet, he never received a young goat to celebrate with his friends. "This brother has wasted your money, comes crawling back home, and you throw a lavish party. It's just not fair." (Paraphrased) The father desired to share great joy, and the son was filled with bitterness and contempt.

Questions to ponder:

☐ What do you think the older son first felt when he saw his younger brother returning home?

_____

☐ Have you ever had a lost family member or even a friend return with a changed heart?

_____

☐ What made the difference in their life?

_____

☐ What do you think the Jewish leaders were feeling or thinking at this point?

_____

☐ Have you ever felt like there has been injustice in your life? If so, how did it make you feel?

_____

The Pharisees felt they had been doing the work of God. They interpreted the scrolls, protected all of the Old Testament laws, and taught the people. They even added to the laws, as they felt justified. That was their job and they were doing it. Jesus came in and seemed to defy the law. He healed on the Sabbath. He went out of his way to teach sinners. The religious leaders were considered the "righteous" ones. For over two hundred years, these men were recognized as the spiritual leaders of Israel. Now, in only about 3 years, Jesus has come and turned their accomplishments upside down. How would you react if your life's work were deemed worthless virtually overnight? They were angry to say the least. How many of them repented and understood, we can only conjecture. One thing is certain, however. Jesus would rejoice with the angels in heaven, if even one got it.

The eldest son was more like the Pharisees and teachers of the law, as his heart was hardened against the father. He felt he was doing everything right. Yet, when his brother returned, he could not share in the celebration. He couldn't relate like the Pharisees, who would not associate with those they deemed lower than them. This brother put himself in that level, when he left and squandered everything. "How dare my wayward brother try to get back in my father's good graces? How dare my father take him back with such an elaborate party? Haven't I done everything asked of me?" These words sound much like the religious leaders who protected and dedicated themselves to the law.

Questions to ponder:

☐ Have you ever known someone who defended his or her position without compromise?

_____

☐ Have you witnessed a person who had a change of heart (or mind) on an issue?

_____

☐ How do you come across to those you meet?

_____

THE PARABLE OF THE SHREWD MANAGER

The parables do not end there.

Luke 16: 1 – 14

1 Jesus told his disciples: "There was a rich man whose manager was accused of wasting his possessions.

2 So he called him in and asked him, 'What is this I hear about you? Give an account of your management, because you cannot be manager any longer.'

3 "The manager said to himself, 'What shall I do now? My master is taking away my job. I'm not strong enough to dig, and I'm ashamed to beg—

4 I know what I'll do so that, when I lose my job here, people will welcome me into their houses.'

5 "So he called in each one of his master's debtors. He asked the first, 'How much do you owe my master?'

6 " 'Eight hundred gallons of olive oil,' he replied. "The manager told him, 'Take your bill, sit down quickly, and make it four hundred.'

7 "Then he asked the second, 'And how much do you owe?'" "'A thousand bushels of wheat,' he replied. "He told him, 'Take your bill and make it eight hundred.'

8 "The master commended the dishonest manager because he had acted shrewdly. For the people of this world are more shrewd in dealing with their own kind than are the people of the light.

9 I tell you, use worldly wealth to gain friends for yourselves, so that when it is gone, you will be welcomed into eternal dwellings.

10 "Whoever can be trusted with very little can also be trusted with much, and whoever is dishonest with very little will also be dishonest with much.

11 So if you have not been trustworthy in handling worldly wealth, who will trust you with true riches?

12 And if you have not been trustworthy with someone else's property, who will give you property of your own?

13 "No servant can serve two masters. Either he will hate the one and love the other, or he will be devoted to the one and despise the other. You cannot serve both God and Money."

14 The Pharisees, who loved money, heard all this and were sneering at Jesus.

15 He said to them, "You are the ones who justify yourselves in the eyes of men, but God knows your hearts. What is highly valued among men is detestable in God's sight.

From one sheep in a hundred to one coin in ten to a father and his two sons, we can see the progression. Now we have two players mentioned. One was a rich man and the other a manager under his employ. The rich employer heard something about his manager that warranted dismissal. We are not told what it was, but we are assured that it was contrary to the desires of his employer. At the end of the last parable we saw the attention turned to the son who remained, and the father's desire for him to rejoice over his brother's return. Now we have a one-on-one confrontation between an owner and a manager. The progression continues.

Upon hearing about his dismissal, the manager made preparations to improve his status by appealing to those under his management. By reducing their debt load the manager would gain favor. Future employers, often, place considerable weight on a good referral from others. Perhaps this manager considered referrals from the new friends, whom he would make through acts of kindness. Perhaps he was thinking about where his next meal would come from, and these friends would welcome him. Nevertheless, he used worldly wealth to attempt to buy favor, wealth that didn't even belong to him.

His master saw what he was doing and commended him for his shrewdness. That seems to be in contrast to the reasons for the manager's firing. Do not confuse shrewdness with wisdom. The manager acted out of self-preservation using earthly influence for earthly gain. The parable goes on to talk about eternal wealth, which cannot be received from earthly desires. The manager focused on things seen, but the lesson of the story was on what is unseen. "People of the light" refers to those who recognized that earthly wealth is fleeting, and true rewards are eternal.

Jesus told them: *"⁹I tell you, use worldly wealth to gain friends for yourselves, so that when it is gone, you will be welcomed into eternal dwellings."* What does that mean to each of us today? The first step is to recognize that we are stewards of what we have. We have nothing when we come into the world, and we will leave the same way. Earthly things are temporary. Therefore, it is important to use these things in ways that will have more lasting value long after we are gone. The manager in the story sought to have his earthly desires fulfilled. Thoughts of the future were on how he could better himself with worldly things like food, shelter, money, and pleasure. He provided debt relief to some, in hopes of payment in kind in the future. He chose those who owed his master the most, for the highest potential payback later. He did not recognize that he was a steward of his master's wealth. In fact he gave away what he did not own.

Second, We need to understand what eternity means along with those things that are to last forever. In today's world we may see the new car, large screen television, or new home as wonderful things to own. But, each of them will pass away someday. Eternity is never-ending. It is the same yesterday, today, and tomorrow. Jesus says, *"Don't store treasures for yourselves here on earth where moths and rust will destroy them. But store your treasures in heaven where they cannot be destroyed by moths or rust and where thieves cannot break in and destroy them. Your heart will be where your treasure is."* (Matt 6: 19-22) Heaven is mentioned as a place where the items we place there are not subject to the worldly destructive influences. That seems to imply that automobiles would never wear out, and clothes would always look as good as the day they were bought. Yet, Jesus was referring to treasures of the heart, which are unseen.

So what are the treasures that we need to store up in heaven? Remember the teachers of the law were listening to Jesus telling these parables. They were considered wealthy and respected members of the church. Their very position in society, as defenders of the law of God, warranted a place in eternity, at least in their eyes. Yet Jesus was also speaking to the multitudes, which were considered lowly in stature by comparison. What could these people possibly have as treasures to store in heaven? Those listening to Jesus' message would not yet understand that our very soul is one treasure desired in heaven, since Jesus was still among them. Yet, today we have the knowledge that Jesus came to live among men and die so that the souls of men could spend eternity with him. During his message, Jesus would refer to sin, forgiveness, faith, and servanthood (Luke 17) as crucial elements for eternal significance. If giving earthly goods to others like food, clothing, or a place to rest produces a desire of their hearts to know about Jesus, then heaven smiles. Leading others to a personal relationship with Christ provides great rejoicing in heaven. We build up treasures in heaven when we share our faith, in the one who created everything, to others. Those on the hillside would learn that they could pass on a legacy of love to their family, friends, and even strangers without having earthly possessions.

Jesus went on to tell them about the love of money as a problem with God. He did not imply that money, by itself, was a problem, but rather the love of it. He referred to money as being a master, and that we cannot have two masters. We will love the one and hate the other. These comments must have struck the very hearts of the Sadducees and Pharisees in the audience, as they held wealth high on their achievement list. Giving up the hold that money had on them would be difficult to be sure. The story was on serving a master. The manager in the story not only lacked wisdom, that the master desired, but he went on to let money lead him on to further destruction.

At the end of the parable Jesus said:

> *"¹³"No servant can serve two masters. Either he will hate the one and love the other, or he will be devoted to the one and despise the other. You cannot serve both God and Money."*

> *¹⁴The Pharisees, who loved money, heard all this and were sneering at Jesus.*

> *¹⁵He said to them, "You are the ones who justify yourselves in the eyes of men, but God knows your hearts. What is highly valued among men is detestable in God's sight."*

The Pharisees sneered at Jesus. The love of money held mastery over them, along with the prestige that came with it. They heard Jesus speak, but the words fell on rocky soil. Their hearts were not penetrated. What about the rest of the audience? Most of them were financially poor. They heard the same message, but with open minds and hearts. Jesus was trying to reach out to them, even as he was reaching out to the spiritual leaders. He spoke about knowing the hearts of men, and He condemned the sin of pride as it applied to worldly wealth.

Jesus carefully selected His words in front of the crowd. He did not refer to these leaders as hypocrites or vipers, as He did on other occasions. He restrained himself in this account. We can surmise that this was intentional due to the crowd's perception and acceptance of the religious leadership. They came to hear the "new kid on the block" speak, but still had loyalty to the leaders there.

The parables began with the leaders murmuring among themselves. Jesus was associating with sinners and tax collectors, considered to be at the bottom of the barrel in society. The Pharisees considered themselves far above these people, as spiritual icons. In their minds, Jesus should have been talking directly to them. They were filled with curiosity and outrage. God couldn't possibly have sent this messenger to talk to the common people, without first approaching the recognized spiritual leadership of the times. Now Jesus was striking at their very hearts with words of condemnation. Jesus defied their role as spiritual leaders. Without a change of heart, money and power would be their masters, which God would certainly detest. Scripture goes on to say that these leaders went away angry. We don't know if any of them had a change of heart later.

Questions to ponder:

☐   Imagine the reaction of the Pharisees as they sneered at Jesus. Do you think they understood the mystery of Jesus' parables?

_____

☐   Imagine the reaction of those in the crowd toward these leaders. Do you think they felt like sneering or some other reaction?

_____

☐   Do you think the crowd was surprised by how Jesus singled out the Pharisees?

_____

☐   Do you think anyone there unlocked the hidden truths

_____

WHAT WOULD JESUS DO?

This is a fundamental question asked by every Christian at some time, often daily. Situations arise that require careful consideration, before we act upon it. Far too often as humans we respond to situations out of emotion, instead of allowing time to formulate proper thoughts. The story of the Prodigal Son goes far beyond a never-ending father's love, a repentant heart, or the ecstasy in heaven. It illustrates in a marvelous way how we are to conduct ourselves in front of both our friends and our enemies.

Key points:

- ☐ Understand your audience

- ☐ Organize your thoughts

- ☐ Don't force your ideas, let them choose

- ☐ Use metaphors or simple illustrations that they can understand / relate to

- ☐ Do not condescend

Understand your audience

How much more can we accomplish if we have a solid understanding of those with whom we are engaged in conversation? The ability to know every heart and mind in an audience is limited to the Creator. We are not mind readers or clairvoyant, though some people claim to have that gift. Therefore, in order to understand others, we need to work at it. This means that we need to listen more and actively seek to understand. Stephen Covey said it best in one of his seven habits (<u>Seven Habits of a Highly Effective Person</u>), when he said: "Seek first to understand, then to be understood." When people recognize that you care about them, they are more willing to pay attention to what you have to offer. In other words, "People don't care how much you know until they know how much you care." These are words we all need to live by.

Let me illustrate. I was returning from England to America after a two-week business trip. I boarded a double-decker bus headed for the airport. The trip would take about an hour and ten minutes, so I decided to take the scenic view above the driver. The next passengers had the same idea, and they sat next to me. We began a conversation with the normal "where are you headed?" question. They were from Texas, but were on route to Africa as Baptist missionaries. I asked them as to what approach worked best, to reach the natives there for Jesus. They answered me with another story. One group of missionaries tried to force their belief on the shepherds, and the message fell on deaf ears. Then a missionary came and noticed their livestock were weak and needed help. He was a veterinarian. He went to thirty different shepherds and asked to set up visitation times to apply his training to help the animals. They agreed. After nine months of improvement with the flocks, a group of thirty men traveled to the missionary's location and said, "You have been helping us with our sheep, now we want to know about this one you call Jesus." Seek first to understand, then to be understood."

Have you ever been in a situation, where you felt that you needed to approach another person on an issue? You knew that the confrontation was inevitable. Everything you would say was rehearsed in your mind. The time and place was also established. I remember a coworker sharing his story. He came home one night and found his wife irate about their daughter's smoking habit. His wife found an empty pack of cigarettes in their daughter's drawer, while putting clean clothes away. Her words spewed out like a script of a movie drama. The evidence was overwhelming against the daughter, and something needed to be done. My friend said that he planned exactly what he would say to his daughter. Her mother and father told her before that they would not tolerate smoking in their house, and now, she would get the message once and for all. After the confrontation and tongue lashing, the daughter replied, "Dad, did you look at the cigarette pack?" Dad told her that he did not. Then she said, "My friend gave me her phone number, and it was the only thing I could find to write on." What a slap on dad's face. Mom did not seek to understand, nor did dad.

Scenarios like this one happen every day. Mom could have approached her daughter with the "innocent before proven guilty" principle. Instead, she let her emotions get the best of her and assumed the worse. She could have gone to her daughter before her husband arrived to confront the issue directly, but chose to pass the responsibility of reprimand to her husband. Neither parent asked their daughter to provide an explanation before lowering the boom. There are always two sides to a story, namely one of perception and another of facts. My friend shared this story with me on route to work the following day. Embarrassment was written on his face, and remorse was in his voice. He used words like "never again" referring to not getting the facts first. He seemed to learn this lesson, but I often wondered if it would last.

With over 35 years in industry, I have seen this principle, properly applied; make a significant impact on organizations. Working in technical training, we see people with a wide range of backgrounds. Software designers tend to absorb the more intense information, while those asked to maintain the equipment may get lost in the translation. It was necessary to develop two uniquely different sets of course material to meet the needs of both groups. Listening to the students provides vital information for future offerings.

Questions to ponder:

☐ Have you ever worked yourself up over time about a perceived problem?

_____

☐ How do you handle discord in your home?

_____

☐ Have you ever asked WWJD before making an initial confrontation?

_____

Organize your thoughts

Jesus took his time getting to the ultimate points that he needed the Pharisees to hear. He started with a parable about sheep, which they may have found more amusing than interesting. Yet, it may well have placed them in a lighter and less critical mood, since it was not antagonistic towards them. It would have been interesting to watch the reaction of those who came to learn from him. Jesus organized his thoughts and carefully delivered his message. We do not read that the Pharisees left more concerned or angry. Perhaps, some of them understood that they needed to repent. Even one repentant heart would have been worth everything.

The proverbial "open mouth and insert foot" applies here. Without careful planning we often fall short. Words spoken without forethought cannot be taken back, and they can leave lasting scars. On one occasion I was asked to complete an electrical project after losing the key engineers. I was a technician, which was a step below an engineer. I had people on the team with higher credentials. One of them I will call Joe. Joe was one of my overseers, when I was a young electrical apprentice. This time, instead of receiving instructions from him, I was now in a position, where he had to get them from me. Joe was several pay grades above me, with at least ten years seniority. Compound that with the fact that three months of lost time needed to, somehow, be recovered to complete the project in the original time period. Every person needed to pull his or her weight. Joe seemed to want to defy my authority.

The team gathered at the work site one Monday morning, at six A.M. Each week would begin with a status meeting, and the goals for the following week would be discussed. The team of electricians reported on what they completed, and what they could expect to accomplish over the next week. As we discussed each day's milestones, I threw out a half dozen concepts as thoughts, each one building on the previous one. These were meant for Joe's ears. After the electricians received their instructions, I turned to Joe and asked if he knew what he needed to accomplish. He said an emphatic "yes" and left. At 11:30 A.M. that morning Joe returned to the room, with an eleven by seventeen sheet of graph paper for my review. The six thoughts that I had, seemingly, thrown up into the air, were captured on that paper, with only one mistake. One by one, Joe and I reviewed each area. I would start with words like "Have you thought about …" Each time he would let me know that he did. When we came to the one flawed area, I asked a question designed to make him focus on the problem, and he, immediately, grabbed the paper away. A few minutes later he returned with a working correction. I told him to run with it. Then I offered whatever support he needed to complete the task. At 3:30 P.M. Joe had a working prototype on the equipment. Joe would have bucked me every step of the way if I handed him the same drawing first. He needed ownership and I needed to give it to him. That day I turned an enemy into a friend. We had no problems afterwards. Joe was even instrumental in getting the project completed on time.

Questions to ponder:

☐ Are you systematic or impulsive, when you approach daily tasks?

_____

☐ What value do you place on effective planning?

_____

☐ Can you name any Bible characters who acted impulsively? (If so, how did God deal with them?)

Don't force ideas. Let them choose.

The story of Joe also fits this category, as people are more comfortable making decisions for themselves, without feeling forced to comply with the ideas of someone else. Human nature desires to feel like part of a solution and not like a robot. Jesus did not give the Pharisees a straightforward and direct answer. He simply started telling parables, each one with a similar message, yet each one uniquely different. The audience needed to draw conclusions based on their interpretations. Jesus could have said, "Now this is the meaning of the story", but he left the task of discernment to each one there.

I picture the typical psychologist probing a patient with questions like, "What do you think is happening?" or "What do you think that means?" The doctor then proceeds to direct the conversation with more questions. It always amazes me how people can get paid a lot of money to simply produce options, without prescribing a specific cure. Even more impressive is when the patient chooses to make a behavior change. At that point the road to recovery becomes clear and straight. A temporary fix might come in the form of a pill, but a lasting one, often, starts with a new internal dialog. We can make the choice to harbor bitterness towards someone who offended us, for example, and cause great distress to ourselves. Or, we can choose to tap God's mercy and find it in our hearts to offer forgiveness. This does not imply that we forget the offense. Rather, we choose to not let it rob us of the joy, which the weeds of bitterness will choke.

The Pharisees needed to change their behavior. Instead of rejecting Jesus and his teachings, they need to choose to believe and repent. Each time a person comes to the realization that they are wrong and seeks to make atonement, heaven rejoices with great joy. Jesus taught this in each parable. Even the Jewish leaders were included. Jesus knew that each listener needed to hear

His words, discern, and make the choice to repent. Each parable provided a neutral setting with a common message of joy. Jesus tugged at each heart without condescending rhetoric. His words needed to get individuals thinking for themselves, unlike the murmuring being done by the religious leaders. Repentance is a personal choice.

When people feel that they are contributors to the ultimate solution, they become productive supporters. When new ideas are placed as directives, rebellion often occurs. Leadership is having the knowledge of how to get the things accomplished, which need to be done, and at the same time getting those who will be participants to enjoy the ride. Ultimately Jesus desires every one to come to a loving relationship with him, but he knows that needs to be our choice. He cannot force repentance on us.

Questions to ponder:

☐ Do you feel empowered by your church leadership?

_____

☐   What can you do to empower others to use their unique gifts to further God's kingdom?

_____

☐ How do you react to new ideas from others?

_____

Keep it simple

Jesus used ordinary illustrations as parables. A lost coin by itself is just an inanimate object. To the owner it was worth every effort to find it. When found, there was great rejoicing. It sounds like a crescendo in music, where the climax is building up to a beautiful conclusion. How often are the simple things producing the most profound outcomes? If Jesus came in the twenty first century and confronted the religious leaders of the day, what illustrations would he employ? Surely, he would not use sheep. Whatever the objects used, the audience would easily relate to the illustration.

Many authors take pride in developing stories with several themes going on simultaneously. Often the picture changes from one realm to another, leaving the readers guessing. Those kinds of books do not appeal to me, but may be exciting to a more avid reader. The parables of Jesus on the surface are very straightforward, and his audience could easily relate to the objects or characters. The eternal message might take some meditation, but that makes it even more amazing. What appears very simple could have deep spiritual long lasting value.

The Bible consists of sixty-six books with the same simple message, namely, "God loves you." God chose man above all other Creation to be the object of his love. We are told in Genesis that we are made "in His image" and set apart. In Revelations, we are informed that Christ will return to claim his "Bride." A marriage consists of a mutual love for one another. Our time on earth is God's used to allow love to be returned. When you get down to the simple truths, we must conclude that God is love.

John 3:16

"For God so loved the world that he gave his one and only Son, that whoever believes in him shall not perish but have eternal life.

Earthly things will pass away, but eternity is forever. The world has even tried to redefine what love is. The simple truth is that God loved us so much that He was willing to die for us. The parables of Jesus were meant to be simple, but full of the one deep spiritual truth that we are so loved by the Creator that heaven rejoices when we open our hearts to Him as well.

Our children can teach us very valuable lessons in the simplest way. Often their responses to something we ask or share with them leaves us speechless. One day I was having a telephone conversation with my grandson, who is six years old. He was into anything scientific including space. He said he learned about planets and our solar system. I asked him if he could name all the planets, and he answered, "No papa. They are already named." Needless to say, I still laugh when I think of his answer. He heard my question a little different than my intention. His response was a profound one. We can use a lot of big words that most people cannot understand to emphasize a point, and turn people away or we can keep it simple. Jesus used the latter.

Questions to ponder:

☐   Have you ever addressed a complex problem only to find a simple solution?

_____

☐   Have the words of a child ever brought simplicity to what may have, otherwise, appeared difficult?

_____

☐   Do your daily actions tend to muddy the waters or quiet them? (Water can be any difficulty, problem concern or perception)

_____

Don't condescend.

The easiest way to turn off someone is to make him or her feel insignificant and low in spirit. Jesus lets us know that we are all sinners, and yet, he came to save us from the penalty of sin, namely, spiritual death, He loves us so much, that he suffered and died for us. He was with the tax collectors and sinners. Somehow, these people were drawn to him. They, certainly, did not come because Jesus made them feel low in spirit.

I used to keep a sign in my office that read, "The best exercise anyone can get is to bend down and help someone else up." Jesus teaches us to serve one another in love. We are not to go around gossiping or seeking others to support our point of view. That is what the Pharisees were doing. Jesus did not lay their haughtiness out on the table for everyone there to see. Although he called them "vipers" on other occasions, in front of this crowd, he sought to teach them through parables. Building others up breaks down walls of separation. Love is a verb. It requires action.

On a career change within a large company, I was sent to a training class to learn a new process. I frantically took notes and threw myself into the learning process. After the first week, the company sent me out with a qualified equipment service technician who pointed out each area of the equipment mentioned in the class. When I returned for the second week of training, I threw most of my notes away. Seeing the equipment made a huge difference. After relocating to the new work site, I decided to write a letter to the head of the organization, pointing out the problems and offering solutions. Those hired outside the company were sent, immediately, out to work with the service person for at least two weeks prior to receiving training. I was transferred from inside the company and did not have that opportunity. As a result, the company was sensitive to the issues and treated transferees like the outside hires.

The account did not end there. I was bored with the work, as it was not challenging. I was able to transfer back as a maintenance electrician. In less than a year I was called up to work in engineering. This was a big leap. When my new supervisor interviewed me, he asked if I knew why I was called to the engineering department. Then he said it was because of a letter I wrote to management, where I pointed out several problem areas, offered possible solutions, and did it without being condescending. Then he added; "That's the kind of person we need here. Now do you know anything about electricity?"

I could have left well enough alone and done my job after the training was over. The week with the equipment service technician, certainly, removed many cobwebs, as far as understanding the equipment. Yet, I took the time to help others who might enter the program as I did. My intent was to improve the process by offering firsthand information to those in charge. Little did I know that my action would change my life later. I went from being bored in the assignment to a very challenging career as an engineer, which I thoroughly enjoyed. Of course I knew something about electricity, but it was my letter that touched the heart of that engineering manager.

There seems to be an unwritten philosophy that people will be elevated above others when they put them down. Jesus taught exactly the opposite. Peter asked him on one occasion, "Who will be the greatest among them in heaven?" Jesus responded with words that implied the least among them would be the greatest. Later, He demonstrated the principle of humility, by kneeling to wash their feet. The problem with putting others down to get a sense of personal uplifting, is that the gap does not change, only the perception. In other words, when we put someone down, we go down with him or her. However, when we lift someone up, we are also lifted up. Jesus said' "If I be lifted up, I will lift all men unto me." This is an extremely important lessen to be learned, especially by Christians.

Jesus was with the lame, the blind, and all others deemed by society as downtrodden. The sick needed help and not the well. The Pharisees needed to learn humility. Their pride made them think they were so much better than everyone else, at least spiritually. The lessons Jesus taught were meant to pierce their hearts from the inside, rather than boldly confronting them. Putting them down, in front of everyone there, would have caused more harm than good. Not only would the Pharisees not heeded his message, but many of the others listening would have been turned off as well. If the sinners and tax collectors wanted to hear condescending remarks, they could have gone to their religious leaders.

Questions to ponder:

☐ Have you ever wondered how you came across to people in your conversation or actions?

_____

☐ If someone told you that you were condescending or they felt hurt by something you said, how would you deal with it?

_____

☐ When you have ideas for change in a church body, how do you approach others to share them?

_____

☐ Have you ever been approached by someone with a condescending spirit? If so, how did they make you feel?

_____

WHERE ARE WE TODAY?

The following poem has been distributed over email, which says a lot about the state of America today and her values. I wonder what Jesus would say about it? Are we worse than Sodom and Gomorrah? (Author unknown)

Now I sit me down in school
Where praying is against the rule
For this great nation under God
Finds mention of Him very odd.

If Scripture now the class recites,
It violates the Bill of Rights.
And anytime my head I bow
Becomes a Federal matter now.

Our hair can be purple, orange or green,
That's no offence; it's a freedom scene.
The law is specific, the law is precise.
Prayers spoken aloud are a serious vice.

For praying in a public hall
Might offend someone with no faith at all
In silence alone we must meditate,
God's name is prohibited by the state.

We're allowed to cuss and dress like freaks,
And pierce our noses, tongues and cheeks.
They've outlawed guns, but FIRST the Bible.
To quote the Good Book makes me liable.

We can elect a pregnant Senior Queen,
And the 'unwed daddy,' our Senior King.
It's "inappropriate" to teach right from wrong,
We're taught that such "judgements" do not belong.

We can get our condoms and birth controls,
Study witchcraft, vampires and totem poles.
But the Ten Commandments are not allowed,
No word of God must reach this crowd.

It's scary here I must confess,
When chaos reigns the school's a mess.
So, Lord, this silent plea I make:
Should I be shot; My soul please take!

Amen

Jesus said:

Luke 9: 26

"If you are ashamed of me, I will be ashamed of you before my Father."

There is an undermining work in the world that seeks to destroy everything that Jesus spoke about over two-thousand years ago. America was founded on those same principles, yet we seem to have lost our way. Jesus went to anyone who would listen, and spoke about things like joy, hope, love, peace, and eternity. These are wonderful things, yet our world is filled with those who kill innocent women and children in defense of their faith. On the other side we have a movement in America that seeks to destroy anything that comes from God. Are we killing ourselves?

Are we worse than Sodom and Gomorrah? In Genesis 18: 16 – 33 Abraham pleaded on behalf of his nephew, Lot, to spare the city of Sodom. He started out begging God to spare the city if fifty righteous people were there and God said he would. Then Abraham became a little bolder and begged to spare the city if forty righteous men were found; then thirty; then twenty; finally ten. Not even ten righteous people could be found. Lot and his family were taken out before the city was destroyed. Removing God from a country blessed, because it was founded on God's principles, is sadly headed towards a similar fate as Sodom. Those who are willing to stand up for Jesus can still make a difference, but they need to stand up. Man cannot defeat evil, but God already has. We need to be like those sinners and tax collectors and learn from Jesus.

My friend and colleague, Ted McGee writes his thoughts on where America has been heading in the following account, which is much like a parable. It uses a simple illustration, but with a deep and profound message.

Cuts Deeply, Like Broken Glass
By Ted McGee

Years ago, I was stationed at the U.S. Naval Station at Guantanamo Bay, Cuba. In times past, sailors stationed there would sit along cliffs drinking from glass bottles. When finished, they would throw the bottles against the rocks and break them. The small sandy beach at the bottom of the cliffs became known as Glass Beach. At first, the broken glass was sharp and capable of cutting deep into an unprotected foot.

As time went by and waves washed ashore, the sharp pieces of glass gradually lost their cutting edge as they rolled back and forth through the sand. Eventually, the glass became smooth and polished, no longer capable of cutting. Beachcombers collected the colorful pieces of glass to be used in mosaics.

Jesus lived and taught during a time the Roman Empire was still in power. His teachings were remarkable. He offered hope to people who only knew of existence and a future to those who only knew of a painful past. His teachings empowered. His words were sharp and cut through the heart.

Thousands of years have passed and the differences in time, culture, and understanding often dull the edge from the words and teachings of Jesus. For example, Jesus' teaching "Blessed are the poor in spirit, for theirs is the kingdom of heaven" has an entirely different meaning for many of us today, than those who first heard Him speak it the first time.

For us, the Beatitudes offer comfort in the face of an uncomforting world. To those who sat on the mountainside and listened, however; the words were sharper, offering more hope than ever imagined in their meager world. Not only do the Beatitudes offer comfort, they offer a pronouncement of happiness and joy. There is promise as well, a positive outcome in the worst of situations. In a world run, mostly, by the powerful and aristocratic, such a pronouncement lifts a great weight from the burdened heart and brings new found freedom.

Today we live in a world that seems to be crumbling. We fight wars on drugs, illiteracy, hunger, disease, and terrorism. At times it seems as if we are pushed beyond the bounds of our resources, and we ask if the Bible still holds promise for us. The answer is simply "Yes." When we are pushed beyond the bounds of our resources, God's resources take over. When viewed in a different light or from a different angle, things hidden from us can suddenly come into view. It isn't really the words and teachings of the Bible that have dulled, but our understanding. With a closer look we can see the Bible cuts as deeply today, as it did when the words were first spoken.

Ted points out that great spiritual erosion has taken place in our world since Jesus walked among us over 2000 years ago. America was founded on good solid Christian principles, and similar erosion has taken place in a much shorter time. The family unit has been compromised. The eighteenth century was marked with hard working families who ate together, worked together, prayed together, and stayed together. The twentieth century began a revolution of change, where affluence and technology started to usurp many of the parenting duties. Television and video games baby-sat children, while mom and dad worked. Fast food took its toll on family dining time, not to mention our waistlines. Money and things seemed to preoccupy the average American family and slowly became idols. Drugs served to preoccupy some into false euphoria, while dulling human senses.

This same affluence also became a driving force in breaking down the family. Psychologists say that money is the number one cause of marriage breakups. The divorce rates in this country are among the highest in the world. The twenty first century has been entered with even more erosion. Credit card dept, depression, and suicide are increasingly adding to the process. Large corporations are downsizing, adding high stress to the workforce and ultimately the family unit. Unemployment also affects churches, as they struggle to meet expenses with the drop in tithes and gifts.

The glass bottles would cut to the bone if they were walked on after they hit the rocks below. Slowly the tides of life started to dull the edges in the same way, as time has hurt the family unit in America. Many countries have maintained their customs and traditions, but here we see them replaced with new ones. Somehow we need to get back to the basics. The things of this world are nothing compared to what awaits in heaven, so why worry about them. Christians need to rekindle their relationships with the Creator and get on with the business of Jesus, namely, spreading his word.

Hebrews 4: 12

For the word of God is living and active. Sharper than any double-edged sword, it penetrates even to dividing soul and spirit, joints and marrow; it judges the thoughts and attitudes of the heart.

The words of Jesus penetrated to the very soul. Once again it needs to cut to the hearts of people and bring them back to a life filled with love, joy, and peace; rather than anger, resentment, and hostility. Men need to be men again and stand up for their beliefs. Families need leadership from within and not from worldly influences. It is interesting that the biggest blockbuster movies coming out of Hollywood are Christian themes. Movie moguls predicted that Mel Gibson's "Passion of the Christ" would be a flop, and last count shows a ten-fold return on Mel's fifty million dollar investment. "The Lion, the Witch, and the Wardrobe" by CS Lewis, released as "The Chronicles of Nardia", has brought in over six hundred million dollars worldwide. The world has shown interest in spiritual things. It needs champions to step up one family at a time.

Questions to ponder:

☐ Does the direction your country is taking appear to be better or worse that the previous century?

_____

☐ The technological advances have changed our world. How have they been beneficial?

_____

☐ What good areas have been removed by technology?

_____

☐ Where are we headed if we stay the present course?

_____

WHAT WILL YOU DO WITH JESUS?

This is the fundamental question being asked by our Father in Heaven today. Each of us needs to search our hearts and answer it. We either need to believe that Jesus was and is who he said he is, namely, God's "one and only son," or we can choose to reject him. To reject him, without closely studying the evidence of his life and followers, can have eternal consequences. Therefore, we all need to approach this question carefully and completely.

Leaders and statesmen have come and gone. Books have recorded most, if not all of their lives, for us to remember and for future generations. Time is the ultimate test. Most of us remember names like Abe Lincoln, Bach, or Einstein because of their contributions. Most of us cannot tell you who won the batting title last year in baseball or the Super bowl MVP two years ago. We get caught up in the moment and quickly fade with time. Baby boomers remember the name of Elvis, but this generation may not. The name of Jesus has passed the test of time. No one in all of history has left such a mark. Nearly all religions recognize that he was a real person, who did extraordinary things.

He claimed to be God in the flesh. Either Jesus was who he said he was or he was a liar. Many doctrines claim that Jesus was a great teacher but not God. How can he have even the title of teacher if he lied about being God? We have to believe he was (and is) the Son of God, or we need to run as far away from him as we can. There doesn't seem to be a middle ground.

Let's look at the writings of those with Jesus, to help us with this decision. These were ordinary men with different backgrounds who took the time to write in their own words the accounts of his life. Try to do that today with a prominent and well-respected personality. We could ask each presidential cabinet member to each write a book about the president. The likelihood that the stories would support each other is probably slim at best. Now have the writers write their accounts after being away from the man for several years. I hope you get the point. The writers of the New Testament were remarkable. Each account painted the same picture, despite their different backgrounds and the timeframes when they penned them. Did Jesus make the difference? Were these men directed by a source beyond their own abilities?

Then we have accounts written hundreds of years before Jesus came, detailing the precise events that would take place. Prophets like Micah spoke of not only the birth but also how he would die. Hundreds of Old Testament verses prepared the way for his New Testament life. That simply cannot be a coincidence. The test of a prophet is that his prophecies are a hundred percent correct, or he is not a true prophet. Prophets are considered God's messengers. If we believe the words of the prophets, then we must believe in the one who sent them. The sixty-six books, written by at least forty different authors, all coming together in a single manuscript have a unity that has confounded the skeptics. How could this be?

Then we need to examine the very lives of those who were close to Jesus, namely his disciples. Peter was weak when he denied knowing Jesus on three occasions. He was impetuous, as he tried to elevate himself above the others. Yet, after the resurrection, he died a martyr's death. He was crucified upside down. This was not the act of a coward, nor was it arrogance. Dying like his savior demonstrated Peter's humility. Dying upside down demonstrated his shame for denying Jesus. This was an act of love beyond human understanding.

Paul met Jesus on the road to Damascus, while He was bent on ending the Christian movement. He was a Pharisee. He was well schooled in the law. He, jealously, pursued and even authorized death to those who defied the Mosaic Laws. Paul's life took a dramatic change, and God used Paul's zeal to become, perhaps, the greatest evangelist in history. Much of his time was spent behind prison walls, yet his letters to the newly formed churches were inspiring. He said, (Phil. 1:21) "For me, to live is Christ and to die is gain". Paul was a changed man because of his encounter with Jesus, filled with love, joy, and hope. If these are things missing in your life, try Jesus. He stands at the door of every heart, waiting for the door to open. (Rev. 3:20) "Here I am! I stand at the door and knock. If anyone hears my voice and opens the door, I will come in and eat with him, and he with me."

Twelve men were chosen to be in the inner circle with Jesus. He talked with them, prayed for them, and personally chose them. They followed willingly and without delay. Upon the death of Jesus, the life of Christ spread throughout the whole world. These men did not go back to their previous lives. They were changed in every way. They did not fear death. The doubts of Thomas were removed forever. They were commanded to go into the entire world and make "Disciples of all Nations" (Matt. 28:19). That was exactly what they did. They did not sit back and wait for Christ's return. They did what they were told and did it with joy.

Earthly wealth will fade away. People will come and go. Yet, we read the last verse in Matthew, which says: "I will never leave you or forsake you.' It was a promise that these men took seriously. It also went beyond time and extends to everyone alive today. Do you desire to know Jesus, experience his love, and have unspeakable joy in your heart? If so try Jesus.

Questions to ponder:

☐ What will you do with Jesus?

_____

☐ If Jesus has been made Lord of you life, are there areas, where you still say are off limits

_____

☐ If Jesus has forgiven you, how do you approach those who offend you?

_____

☐   Has this study changed the way you handle relationships with family members?

_____

☐ …with co-workers?

_____

☐ …with members of your congregation?

_____

☐ …with strangers?

_____

☐ …with Jesus?

_____

Author, Dennis A. McIntyre, welcomes any feedback.
Feel free to contact him at:

dennismcintyre6@gmail.com

www.ingramcontent.com/pod-product-compliance
Lightning Source LLC
Chambersburg PA
CBHW021650120626
46545CB00002B/797